Content Marketing for Lawyers

Content Marketing for Lawyers

*How Attorneys Can Use
Social Media Strategies to Attract
More Clients and Become Legal
Thought Leaders*

Michele Ruiz

Contents

Acknowledgments

Much like content marketing and social media, writing a book such as this and all the resources that accompany it take a community. A special thanks to my treasured team who helped make this book a reality.

First, thank you to Gisella Gorman who helped bring structure to my thoughts and pulled it together into a readable manuscript. Thanks to Alex Manriquez for researching, fact-checking and adding her social media insights. I truly appreciate my book writing coach, Alicia Dunams, who convinced me as a subject matter expert to write this book, provided me a process to get it done smartly, and was pleasantly persistent in making sure it actually got done while I've been managing a growing business. Thank you to my book editor Patti McKenna and her wordsmithing magic.

Many thanks go to legal thought leader Peter Zeughauser who supported the idea of this book and was instrumental in some early ideation for the content herein. To my incredibly supportive team at Ruiz Strategies - Esmeralda Ramirez-Rueda, Schenae' Rourk, Nicole Childers, Briana Manrique, Cherie Shepherd, Maria Nork, Deryk Lanier and others, you're the absolute best.

And to my darling children who never once complained about finding me at the computer working late into the evening and showing tremendous understanding for my demanding entrepreneurial life - I love you both beyond measure.

Foreword

"Powerfully" is the only way to describe how Michele Ruiz weaves together her formidable communications and marketing skills and insights to describe the rapid emergence of content marketing and social media at the vortex of legal marketing. In doing so, she concisely makes the case that every lawyer and law firm must make use of the arsenal of digital tools to communicate the value they can deliver as an essential component in their go-to market strategy. If you need to know more about why this is so, or what to do about it and how, or if you feel compelled to convince someone else in your firm of it, whether you are the chair or managing partner of a large or small law firm, a law student, an associate, a young or senior partner, or just flying solo, or if you are reporting to someone in the C-suite, this book will lay it all out for you in an hour or two, from the predicate for, or the "how-to" of, content marketing and social media for lawyers and law firms.

If you believe that developing and retaining the best clients for the best work and ultimately building trusted advisor relationships is about delivering value *in addition to being a great lawyer,* this book is the accelerator you need to get from 0 to 100 and beyond, fast. Fair warning: it does not portend to be a substitute for tried-and-true relationship-based marketing and business development: networking, publishing, speaking, serving as a "go-to" source for journalists or even letting your results speak for themselves. Instead, recognizing that rare is the ultra-successful lawyer who has enough time to spend on building all the business he or she can, Michele explains in easy-to-understand steps dozens of ways you can use social media to leverage your relationship building and business development time without getting lost in jargon or overwhelmed by options and avoid being bested from the "short list" by a competitor because a prospect had never heard of you or the value you deliver.

Every minute of every day we rely on more and more data for everything we do. When was the last time you pulled a volume of an encyclopedia off your book shelf? Instead, we entered the era of the Internet. We use our cell phones, our tablets, and our PCs to search data on the cloud for answers to nearly all of our questions. Yes, Virginia, legal marketing data indicates that prospects and clients increasingly turn to the cloud to find the expertise they need. If you're not on the Internet, clients can't find you. If they can't find you, they can't hire you. Likewise, the brighter the value you deliver shines, the more places it will go, the more likely you will be found, and the better clients will understand why they need you on their short list. This is the essence of content marketing. It is upon us now, and it is our future.

Ultra-successful lawyers and law firms are always looking for ways to turn their expertise into great results to build strong relationships and win more work. If that's you, or if you're interested in joining them at the top, this book is bound for you. It may well be the most valuable business development book you will ever read. Enjoy the success it will bring you!

Peter Zeughauser
Zeughauser Group

Introduction

We are going through the biggest revolution in the way people communicate since the invention of television. Legal marketing is changing because your clients and potential clients have already changed. The Internet, social media, and the Smartphone have created new expectations. There is an expectation of knowing more about you as a lawyer than just the firm you're with, where you went to law school, how many years you've been practicing, and what cases you've successfully prosecuted or defended. Think your profile on your firm website is enough? Not anymore.

Today's clients are more sophisticated and highly informed. The Smartphone has made information available at our fingertips at any time, no matter where we are. Much of the information that influences how potential clients choose a lawyer like you is based on content found online via search engines, websites, and most often social media. And if there is no or little information about you online, you might as well be invisible. And if the content people find about you online is comprised of reviews, that happen to be negative, you are not going to be perceived as a good lawyer.

The lawyers who have lots of quality content online and an effective social media strategy to distribute that content are building their personal brand and a strong book of business effectively and cost-efficiently, and they are winning clients over their competition.

You have heard of social media marketing. The fuel for a good business development strategy using social media is content- yours and other people's content. Blogs, videos, podcasts, eBooks, virtual events, white papers, infographics, online brochures, press releases, PDFs, PowerPoints, and SlideShares are just some examples of content.

Besides your website, a key way to get that content out and communicate directly with your target clients is through social media platforms—Facebook, LinkedIn, YouTube, Twitter, Instagram, Pinterest, and others. And when you produce or share good content – high quality, valuable, helpful, interesting information – your online friends, fans, connections, and tweeps (Twitter followers) will share your content to their online friends, fans, connections, and tweeps, and that's how you leverage your social networks.

As a professional storyteller, I can tell you that while this may sound complicated and hard, this book and the bonus content online at www. MicheleRuiz.com will show you how to produce high-quality content like a pro. Seriously. I'm a former TV journalist, and I'm sharing insider secrets so you can easily, confidently, and frequently create and publish content your target clients want to read, watch, and know about.

Here's your first tip – creating valuable content is a key way to get PR these days because editors, reporters, and influential bloggers decide what to report on and who to include as experts, largely based on the information they find about you online. This includes your social profiles, your content, and, importantly, what others are saying about you on the web.

The secrets I'm sharing with you in this book are organized into two parts. Part I includes the need to embrace content marketing, dispelling common misconceptions, the benefits of a strategy, examples of how other lawyers and law firms are achieving success, how to persuade your partners if they aren't on-board with a social strategy, some information on the legal risks – real and perceived, and the trend of every person now being their own brand. Yes, even you.

Part II offers the detailed "how-to" guidance, starting with an explanation of the most widely-used social media platforms today, social media basics, content creation and how to get started, developing a content marketing and social media strategy, top mistakes to avoid, and time-saving techniques. Plus, I've included 25 impactful content ideas to get you started that can be adapted no matter what type of law you practice. And since the social media platforms change often (think how often Facebook has changed in the last few years), there are supplementary videos, templates, and guides online where the most updated "know-how" will be available to you.

I've created a special resource for you. Go to www.MicheleRuiz.com/ContentMarketingResources.

This book and the online resources will show you exactly what you need to know, in concise, easy-to-understand formats so you can deepen your relationship with current clients, attract new clients, and become a thought leader so you are top of mind and the "go-to" attorney. If you're not sure about this, don't worry. I've included some of the best examples of lawyers and law firms that are building their book of business and reaching new clients through the use of content marketing combined with social media strategies. If they can do it, so can you. Remember, the best thing about this is that most of your competitors probably don't even know these secrets yet.

Michele Ruiz
www.MicheleRuiz.com
Twitter: @MicheleRuiz01
Facebook: Michele Ruiz
LinkedIn: Michele Ruiz
Google+: Michele Ruiz
Instagram: Michele Ruiz

Part 1
The Case for Content
Marketing and Social Media

1 How Content and Social Media Marketing Really Works for Lawyers

A few years ago, I was preparing my business to work with the federal government and had a few questions about teaming agreements, knowing they are commonly used. What are they? I wanted to see examples. I wanted to know what I should be aware of when teaming with another company. Similar to millions of people, I went online and searched for information about teaming agreements. My search turned up a PDF of a PowerPoint called "What Is a Teaming Agreement?" I'd found exactly the information I needed.

My quest continued: this PowerPoint presentation was put together by a law firm in Washington, D.C. It was obviously created for an in-person presentation; however it had enough information that I realized there was much I needed to be aware of before entering into this type of agreement. While I wasn't initially looking for a lawyer, I realized I was likely going to need some legal guidance. The PDF of the PowerPoint wisely included the contact information for the law firm. I copied the link into my browser and landed on their home page, which highlighted they are federal government contracts attorneys.

Within a short five minutes, that law firm had my attention and had answered some of my crucial questions, simply with their content on the Internet. I poked around on their site, glanced at their Publications section, and went to the attorney profiles section and read about the four partners. From there, I proceeded to LinkedIn and looked up the firm to see if I knew anyone who knew them and, if so, had they been recommended. I read some positive recommendations about how helpful the firm had been to other business owners. I sent an InMail (the equivalent of an email via LinkedIn) to one of the law firm partners. I let him know a bit about the potential teaming arrangement I was considering, that I had some questions and asked if he could be of assistance.

With no active effort, this lawyer had picked up a new client within three days. Remember, I didn't set out looking for an attorney. I didn't know about this firm, nor the lawyer. No one at the firm had ever met me. I simply followed the same path millions of potential clients follow. I had some questions and went online to find answers. The scenario I just described above is the power of content marketing at work.

Why Old Marketing isn't Enough in Today's Digital Age

Before the advent of the Internet and social media, lawyers traditionally focused on a number of methods to drive business development. First and foremost, this has been through serving their clients well and reaping the benefits of referrals based on that good performance. This time-honored method, of course, continues today, but given the large number of competing firms and services like Legal Zoom vying for a limited pool of potential clients, solely relying on this method can be challenging in today's evolving legal environment.

Press releases are another marketing tool commonly employed today, with the release covering large case wins or other news or information that is relevant to current or potential clients. The challenge here lies in your target clients actually seeing the press release in an overloaded online world. Additionally, influencing news organizations or publications to deem a particular press release worthy of reporting that story is often difficult.

Networking and attending industry events are standard operating marketing methods for lawyers as well, assuming potential clients take the time to engage with the ever-growing number of attorneys looking to win their business. Lastly, in some states, attorneys are able to advertise directly on radio, television, and billboards. These can be effective but also costly and may not provide a great return on investment.

So, why change course you might ask? In many cases, these methods have worked and continue to work for attorneys to grow revenue at a steady pace. In short, the answer is the Internet. Before the web and now social media, you had limited marketing options – referrals, networking, holding seminars, buying advertising or getting media coverage. Today, lawyers have the ability to tell their story and reach thousands of potential clients in a very targeted online environment—all while spending a LOT LESS on advertising, if anything at all, and not having to hope a reporter will write a piece about them.

The most cost-efficient and time-saving marketing, advertising, and PR strategies today are not what have been done traditionally. It's a new world, with new technologies and new client expectations.

Potential clients want to understand why you as a lawyer are the right person to solve their problem or to help them through their issue. They are not necessarily interested in the one-way message traditional advertising provides. Information seekers want to understand more of your unique subject matter expertise and know a little bit about you as a person. Online channels and strategies provide these in-depth connections and answers at user's fingertips, rendering the traditional methods of attraction less effective.

With the advent of Smartphones and tablets, potential clients use the Internet, everywhere and all of the time, for answering even the simplest of questions or seeking solutions to a problem. Think about the power of a user finding helpful information put out by you that answers their immediate question. This useful information is in the form of digital content. The information seeker stumbles upon your blog, your SlideShare, or your fully completed LinkedIn profile, and finds the answer he or she seeks. They may not have even been looking for a lawyer, or if they were, it was your content that gave them the confidence that you might be able to help them influencing them to learn more about you.

Statistics show that when researching a potential lawyer or a law firm to hire, potential clients will often look online, including at social media and your website.[1] Even when they are referred by someone they trust, they will surely research who you are, and that might well be at 1 o'clock in the morning. The old or traditional ways are becoming increasingly less effective. Savvy lawyers have changed their strategies to keep up with the digital revolution, spending less time and resources marketing for, oftentimes, better results.

Attorneys and law firms that are not online, fully engaged developing digital content, or active in social media are missing out on tremendous opportunities. According to a LexisNexis® Martindale-Hubbell® study, more than 75 percent of people looking for lawyers or legal advice initially turn to the web for information.[2] Alternatively, in states where lawyers have been able to advertise through more traditional channels, such as television and radio, consumers intuitively perceive the information as marketing speak or even, in some instances, propaganda, and thus have been shown to be statistically less affected and engaged with the marketing message and intent.

2 What Exactly is "New Marketing"?

Technology and social media have changed what influences clients to consider you as the lawyer to go to. They read online reviews, they look to see who they know through social media and who knows you, they check your LinkedIn profile to see if you have one and what it says, they delve into content you may be featured in or created yourself and then maybe they may also check your website. Everything I just described and more falls under what is often called "new marketing".

What Exactly is Social Media, Social Networking, Social Media Marketing, and Content Marketing?

Various words and phrases commonly used when referring to new marketing can be confusing. Below are some you might hear and what they mean.

Social media as a marketing phrase can encompass a great deal. There are numerous technologies and platforms available today that allow people to share thoughts, images, and comments, gather online, and create communities. Through actions such as sharing or liking content on Facebook, millions of people are communicating and connecting on the web.

As of this writing, the most popular social media platforms people are using to interact online are Facebook, Twitter, LinkedIn, Instagram, and Pinterest. YouTube and mobile apps (applications that are downloaded to mobile devices) are sometimes included in the definition of social media as they are also technologies that provide opportunities to communicate directly with your target audience online - in other words be "social."

You may have heard the term **"social networking,"** which starts with a person filling out a profile on at least one social platform and using that platform to connect, engage, or communicate with others online.

The broader term **"social media marketing"** refers to a well thought-out, purposeful strategy on how to use social media to achieve certain business objectives, then using measurement and analytics to evaluate whether those objectives are achieved. It involves high-level strategic thinking with key stakeholders in your firm and defining very specifically what the business objectives should be. These goals might include higher revenue, increased brand awareness, speaking opportunities, getting X number of new potential clients to download an eBook, or other specific outcomes. There are online tools, as well as offline methods, that can be used to measure the effectiveness of the strategy against the business objectives.

"Content marketing" is the glue that keeps all of these elements together. It is defined as creating, publishing, and sharing content such as blogs, videos, PowerPoints, and more (usually online) in order to achieve specific goals. Through content marketing, you provide value to your target client by answering questions, providing insights, sharing "how-to" information, or creating some other type of content that your ideal client finds valuable. To be clear, the purpose of content marketing is NOT to spread a "this is what we do and why we're the best at it" message. Rather, when thinking from your potential clients' perspective, you should be providing them helpful information that answers their needs or solves their problems.

"Inbound marketing" is the use of strategies to pull people to you through social media marketing, link building, SEO, blogging, email newsletters, videos, case studies and other tactics to attract potential clients to your website.

Why Content Marketing Strategies Help Grow Your Practice

A powerful content marketing strategy will employ online content that is highly valuable and pulls clients toward you at the exact moment they're looking to solve a problem. One good example of this strategy in action can be seen through Dan Harris, an internationally-regarded legal authority on conducting business in China. He frequently writes blogs on topics related to Chinese law and protecting foreign businesses in their Chinese operations. The content he creates is published and shared via social media platforms such as LinkedIn, proving to be an effective strategy in aiding Dan to build his book of business. These online tactics of social networking and creating a content strategy are parts of the whole and ideally are interrelated, encompassing together what is called Social Media Marketing.

To get to that point, attorneys and law firms must first make sure they are easily and readily found online. This involves search engine optimization, a campaign that will be discussed in greater depth in this book. To sum it up though, the more unique pieces of content you post online that link back to your website (inbound links), the higher your search engine ranking will be. A higher ranking means your website will rank higher when potential clients search the Internet; therefore, more people are likely to visit your website. For these reasons, it is important to create good quality content that has value to your readers.

We exist in an age that is information-driven with individuals who are constantly looking for more. It used to be that having a website presence of any kind was enough in terms of an online presence, however that's not the case any longer. Consumers expect to find a well-developed website, including practicing lawyers' bios and their individual areas of practice, firm location, and other standard information on every law firm's website, not just those that are larger and more well-known. These bits of online information are simply the entry fee into the race, and by far not the winning ticket.

Deeper, more engaging content which you or your firm have published gives the potential client a sense that you are qualified or have the right expertise to solve the issues at hand, which is what is called for to win this race. Traditional methods of marketing simply do not answer this call.

Traditional Marketing is Not Over

This is not to say there is not a place in your arsenal for more traditional methods of reaching potential clients. However, applying digital strategies to support and bolster the effectiveness of those "tried and true methods," presuming, of course, that they are still cost-efficient and deliver the highest return on investment, is using the best of both worlds to effectively reach your next client. The outlier here is the value of your time—the time you put into marketing yourself and your firm.

Attending an event in order to network with potential clients for the purpose of developing a relationship takes time, and lots of it. Digital strategies and social media (think contributing and engaging in big LinkedIn groups focused on legal matters and other such ideas) are non-traditional "networking events" held online, thus being much more targeted and certainly more time efficient in terms of building relationships.

Traditional advertising channels, in the states that allow legal advertising, can be very costly. Digital strategies are much more cost effective and very tightly targeted, therefore, delivering a higher return on your investment. More and more law firms today are committed to ramping up their social media presence and content marketing efforts as they begin to realize this benefit.

In the past, "broadcasting" your message in any meaningful way typically meant relying on a press release or media outreach strategy. Most messages were developed around a notable case win, a particularly exciting new hire, or the establishment of a new practice department in the firm. Once the release was distributed, the next step was hoping that some news organization or publication would find the information newsworthy and publish it. Getting the message out was largely reliant on other parties and their willingness to participate.

Now, with digital strategies, and with social media in particular, you are in complete control of your message and the breadth of its coverage. With the simple posting of a blog, press release, or an announcement and pushed out using social media you can reach a targeted audience yourself without having to rely on the press or any other entity's involvement to get your message out. You are in control of your message and have the ability to release it at any point in the time frame you desire. That shift in control is powerful.

Social media is also very powerful because it allows you to build relationships and establish yourself as a thought leader in your industry. In the past, someone else of authority had to deem you qualified as a thought leader. While this external recognition remains important and relevant today, a large part of this determination that you are, indeed, a "thought leader" now comes from the content and information you are publishing online and the story you tell about your subject matter expertise, yourself as a lawyer, and your firm.

Social media has become a means for the most extraordinary communication. If Facebook and Twitter can be the catalyst communication tools used to overturn a government in Egypt, in the event known as "Arab Spring," imagine what it can do for your practice. We now have the ability to motivate, persuade, and influence target clients through social media, an ability that never existed to this degree prior to the digital explosion of our age.

Additionally, you are now able to build trust in ways that weren't available before. In the past, one-to-one interpersonal interaction fostered trust between lawyer and client. Today, you can publish blogs that cover topics in which you are a subject matter expert and answer a question or suggest answers to a problem for a target client. The nature of online information is such that as the user reads relevant blog posts by you, their inherent opinion of your knowledge of the issue becomes much more favorable, and you're able to establish credibility through it. As the person who has a legal question reads your blogs and postings, your content will confirm that you are, in fact, a subject matter expert and you can immediately establish trust with potential clients.

More generically, the opportunity to build relationships and connect with numerous people online through social media—be it LinkedIn or Facebook or even micro-blogging on Twitter—is tremendous. You can readily exchange information and provide help or relevant or useful advice to potential clients through your social media network. The seeds of a relationship grow, and potentially that relationship goes offline, via a phone call, an in-person meeting or lunch, or a connection at some event or similar opportunity. This seamless and natural building of relationships is a huge bonus that comes from the use of this much more targeted, time efficient and powerful communication tool.

Ultimately, the ideal scenario is a well thought-out and balanced strategy that uses traditional and newer digital technologies in concert, working together to garner the benefits that each can offer. Referrals, networking, press releases, and inclusion as a thought leader in both speaking events and written materials are all strong ways to build your legal practice. And all of these can be successfully gained or participated in through both traditional and digital methods. The key is to find the right recipe for each that drives your business forward in the most efficient and effective way.

3 Why Lawyers Should Use Content Marketing and Digital Strategies

According to the 2015 *ABA Legal Technology Survey Report*, 62 percent of law firms and 78 percent of lawyers have at least one social media profile. The reasons are for career purposes, education/current awareness, networking, case investigation and client development. 35 percent report having obtained clients from their social media activities.[3]

The digital era has made everyone a publisher. That includes lawyers according to the *2014 State of Digital and Content Marketing Survey* by the Zeughauser Group, Greentarget, and the American Lawyer.[4]

Beyond that, with the growing adoption of social media, you should assume people are talking about you and your law firm on social media platforms and online. You may not readily see or hear it if you're not engaged in the social conversation, but you can be sure it's happening. If you're not telling your story via social media, then others will via reviews, comments, or blogs—and if you're not involved in that conversation, it will be out of your control. It's critical to understand that your story is being told whether or not you are involved. It is far better for you to steer the boat and ensure the story that you want told about your practice, your law firm, and your reputation is the prevalent one.

It is inevitable that someone will have something negative to say about a law firm or a particular lawyer and you must be prepared for it. With content marketing and even social media marketing, you have the ability to address these issues head on, quickly, and in a public forum—often before it gets out of control or creates perceptions that can be challenging to change.

Setting up tools to ensure that you're alerted of what's being said about you online is one key step in staying ahead of this issue. (I have more on that in a later chapter.) Responding to complaints or issues quickly adds immense credibility to your reputation and potential clients' impression of you, both in good, as well as not so pleasant, situations.

Influencing and even correcting the perception about you online is critical. According to a Nielson report, 92 percent of people trust referrals from their family and friends and connections on social media more than they trust what a business says about itself. They also weigh reviews (for example on Yelp or Lawyers.com) more heavily than what you might say about yourself,[5] so "listening" via social for reputation management becomes very important.

One of the most compelling benefits of using social media marketing, for those in the legal profession particularly is the efficiencies it provides to an already time-burdened schedule. Much of the work required to market and build your business via social media can be considered "digital networking," which can be done without leaving your office. Think of the amount of time you might spend at in-person networking events with the goal of meeting potential clients. The beauty of online networking is that a very similar connection can be gained via LinkedIn or Twitter by providing information that the user finds valuable, without the other party feeling as if there is something expected of them in return or that you are attempting to overtly pitch them to use your services. This non-pressured environment readily breaks down the barriers to building relationships.

Another attractive benefit of social media marketing is the increased perception of you and/or your firm as a source for needed information. Content such as blogs, video blogs, white papers, etc., all reinforce your personal brand and your firm's brand as a trusted resource that users can go to when they need answers.

A third notable benefit of using social media is the more automated building of a referral base. Our audience isn't always solely the individual we're talking with at the time. That person's connections can be an invaluable pool of potential clients as well. As mentioned before, if you're pushing out content that's relevant and useful, a user may see it and then refer someone in their circle who they feel could use your services.

Social media is a key way to market. An increasing number of law firms have identified social media as a game-changer for legal marketing. Not only that, but a few lawyers have used it to tell their clients story, and in the process market themselves. Consider Mark O'Mara, former prosecutor and TV legal analyst. He represented George Zimmerman, the man charged in the death of 17-year-old Trayvon Martin. O'Mara's firm launched a social media strategy using a Facebook page, a Twitter account and a blog posting, "We feel it would be irresponsible to ignore the robust online conversation, and we feel equally as strong about establishing a professional, responsible, and ethical approach to new media." The blog explained the purpose was to dispute wrong information, provide a way to communicate with the law firm, a voice for Zimmerman and a way to raise money for his defense.

When Zimmerman surrendered, the firm announced it via Twitter, by-passing the media and other traditional methods of disseminating information about the case. Using social media to get your message our directly to the public is a way to attempt to control the message. According to O'Mara, "social media will become a standard part of the legal process".[6]

> Content, online strategies and social media marketing work together for a targeted and effective integrated approach.

As many are well aware, legal marketing is very competitive. Through the use of social media and an integrated approach across platforms, sub-stantially less can be spent to market your legal services when compared to traditional advertising or primarily offline efforts. The advent of content marketing and social media has made it possible for any lawyer or a law firm of any size to be able to market their services and legal expertise to the masses. Comparatively, prior to digital marketing, having this kind of impact and reach was only available to well-established law firms with much larger budgets and dominance of market share.

When using online marketing, it should be seen as two strategies—"push" and "pull." Push marketing is literally pushing out information to a specified target audience. For example, you might be publishing a blog and posting it in a LinkedIn group that's comprised of people who could be potential clients.

Pull marketing takes the opposite approach. This encompasses strategies to make sure your content is present in the pool of choices a user might "fish" in, either via a search engine results page on Google or Bing, or a social media search when looking for an answer or a service provider. The goal of pull marketing is to get clients to come to you. As a lawyer, you want to be found when someone is looking for a solution, ideally at the top of search engine results. Relevant content is king for search engines, and building an arsenal of content that can be readily found when a user searches on the Internet for key services you offer is paramount.

Content also helps with strategies for being found when potential clients don't know you by name. Some clients you'll have in the next 12 months likely don't currently know you exist. The beauty of digital content is that it appears readily in search engine results or social platforms like LinkedIn for the key services and information you include in your content, not simply for your name or your firm's name. For this reason, content marketing becomes very important, as you want to consistently appear when clients search for solutions that you might be perfectly suited to help solve, but they don't happen to know of you.

Ultimately, we should fish where the fish are plentiful, and clients today have come to expect that they will find information about you online. It is no longer enough in many instances to get a referral. That's a great place to start, and people instinctively trust resources and referrals from friends or trusted colleagues, but word of mouth is no longer the only important screening criteria. A referral is followed almost immediately by online research about you. Therefore, your online presence should reinforce the strong positive momentum taking place at that critical moment.

Business development is based on relationships—relationships that are built over time with an element of trust as a foundation. Social media is one of the best ways to build your reputation as a thought leader, which in turn leads to trust by those seeing your content. That trust, in tandem with the community and relationship-building nature of social media, make it a perfect fit, well suited for your needs in your business development strategy.

What it is Costing You to NOT be on Social Media

The adoption of mobile technology has changed the way people evaluate and make decisions about who they do business with, including deciding who they will trust in such an important role as an attorney. Potential clients are accustomed to jumping on their Smartphones and looking up information about possible lawyers they may want to hire. There's also an expectation that you're going to be active on social media. For all of these reasons, social media marketing is essential for attorneys.

On the flip side, there is a huge downside in not understanding social media. You have those who just "don't get it"—who might know of it, maybe have heard of colleagues, friends, or family members who use it, but ultimately don't really comprehend the usage of social media. Others may be more aware of it, but don't participate for marketing purposes. The downside to these positions in the legal marketing context is that even if you don't understand social media or have chosen not to use it, your competition and your clients do understand it and are using it.

Is there a downside if you still aren't convinced social media marketing is right for you? Basically, if you're not online, you're invisible. While you may not believe yet that its usage is important to you or the growth of your practice, you can bet that much of your competition does. Many times, clients come to lawyers because they have a problem or want to prevent one, and their first step in this process is to do an online search as I did when looking for a government contracts lawyer. If you're not visible or simply have a website but no other online presence, and another law firm that could be an option for that potential client has much more than a website available for them to review and consider, you will likely lose out.

Consider this scenario – your competition has content about particular areas of interest—real estate, venture capital, human resources law, employment law, or whatever the case might be. Competitive law firms will have blogs, videos, white papers, eBooks, and other information related to the areas of interest available online. Your simple website does not sell your experiences, credibility, or skills nearly as well as the other law firms' content arsenal. The likelihood of winning the potential client is much less when they can see that another law firm positions themselves as real subject matter experts.

Additionally, we as consumers are becoming more and more accustomed to getting our information through social media first, rather than initially going to a company's website initially. Your website is critical in your marketing process, but it's not implausible that social media will soon be driving more traffic than any other source, even more than search engines like Google, Yahoo or Bing.

More and more people use online resources when looking for an attorney and that trend is increasing. If you're not visible in numerous places on the web, you're either not going to be found by potential clients or be able to convince them you're THE lawyer to go to.

Attracting Your Future Workforce

Another benefit of social media is the attraction of millennials and other young, very socially adept users. The use of social media draws a line in the sand in many cases ... separating those who do use it and those who don't. When building your winning team of associates and attorneys, you can be sure that those potential employees will review and make note of how "social" your law firm is. Being "socially savvy" will go a long way in recruiting wonderful, qualified young lawyers to your law firm. There is an impression that if you're not on social media or don't understand it, that you're old fashioned—that in and of itself can be a negative. In terms of recruiting both clients and employees, social media is a tool you can't live without.

Adapt or Die: The New Rules of Client Communications

Clients expect that you will be where they are, available to them and ready to serve their needs. Prior to mobile devices and the introduction of constant connectedness, consumers knew when they could and should reach you as a service provider. Typically, that was from 9 to 5, Monday through Friday. In stark contrast, today there is a prevalent perception that even if you are out of the office, you are still reachable and are able to respond.

Clients have gotten to the point where they expect responses to communications, regardless if you are out of the office or not. Being in court notwithstanding, clients today expect that you will receive their email or communication and respond within a reasonable time period, which most often means within hours. This phenomenon forced more and more attorneys to start using of Blackberries and respond to emails and messages, even on the weekends, in some instances.

Much like this adaptation to a new set of rules, the adaptation of mobile technologies is no different with social media. Clients expect more from you and your firm in this age of social connectedness. An ever increasing number of your potential and existing clients are using social media. They're in it, they're involved, they're engaged, and they have an expectation that you will be, as well.

In other words, you need to be where your clients are. You can't expect that they are going to adapt to how you market or communicate information. If your clients are using social media, you need to be there right alongside them. If you're not, eventually they will gravitate to those who are.

The Move-the-Needle Benefits

Using a smart content strategy can move the needle on revenue generation – both in the number of new clients that you attract, as well as the retention of current clients.

Client acquisition using content marketing and social media should be looked at as a sales funnel.

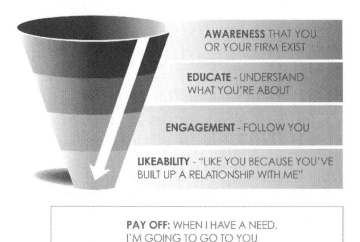

AWARENESS THAT YOU OR YOUR FIRM EXIST

EDUCATE - UNDERSTAND WHAT YOU'RE ABOUT

ENGAGEMENT - FOLLOW YOU

LIKEABILITY - "LIKE YOU BECAUSE YOU'VE BUILT UP A RELATIONSHIP WITH ME"

PAY OFF: WHEN I HAVE A NEED, I'M GOING TO GO TO YOU

The number of potential clients that enter the top of your business development funnel by reading and engaging with some piece of content you've created can be significant. Think of it like this: The potential client enters the top of the funnel because you are creating awareness about you and your services. If you have information that is relevant or of interest to them, you are now educating them, and in return, they get a greater understanding of what you're about.

Once you've convinced a potential client that the information you're providing is valuable, they will likely self-select to follow information that you're pushing out. Now that they are further down the funnel, they are engaged. This step begins a relationship with this potential client as they develop a level of trust about you and your knowledge. At this point, "likeability" comes into play. This trust cannot be underestimated, because once it is established, when a need arises, that potential client will come to you or refer someone who can benefit from your expertise. This all may happen without ever having met you in person. That's often the client acquisition cycle with social media marketing in today's new media world.

Speaking opportunities are another classic way to build your book of business. Content marketing can create opportunities to present your expertise at an event. This is also referred to as educational marketing, which is either holding seminars or speaking at events that are educational or informational about topics relevant to target clients. This type of marketing is very common, either via traditional delivery methods, such as speaking at a conference or digitally by hosting a webinar or publishing an eBook.

There are people who are looking for speakers for particular seminars or events, and your online content results in a much higher likelihood that you will be discovered and asked to speak. Any such speaking engagement extends your business development strategies and pool of potential new clients. All of that is driven through the quality content you upload for the online community to engage with. This is also another way to develop trust with your potential client.

Along this same vein, bloggers, journalists, and editors are always looking for specialists to include in news coverage, whether it be in a very targeted magazine or a much broader publication, such as the *New York Times*. When your online content speaks to your area of expertise, the potential that you will be tapped as an expert to include or quote in a story can grow exponentially. Media coverage elevates awareness about your practice and supports your business development strategies.

Client Retention

As law firms have been struggling in recent years with client retention and changes that have impacted demand for legal services, some have implemented content marketing strategies to help not only attract clients, but to help retain clients. As many of them continue to question the value of paying high billing rates and look to low-cost providers and solutions, publishing regular blogs, videos or vlogs, white papers, and other content that is valuable to clients can effectively serve to stay top of mind and reinforce your value.

Some provide insights, "need-to-know" information, analysis, case studies and other high value content only for the firm's clients. Others provide it to anyone who signs up to receive it. These are not strategies effectively used for the most part by lower cost providers and therefore can provide you with a competitive advantage.

Quality content that is client-centric, helps a client with their needs or concerns, and avoids heavy promotional language can also help justify your fee structure in an environment when clients are more apt to demand write-downs or write-offs. Regularly creating content and pushing it out to your clients is also a way to have a high value touch point with them, and a way to nurture the relationship.

The key is to make sure you have a strategy for creating the content, and a way to measure its effectiveness. I go into that in Part II.

But Aren't There Legal Risks to Using Social Media?

In many instances, lawyers are concerned about the use of social media and the best way to balance the concerns, risks, and benefits of participation.

Typically, the most frequent concerns include:

- Am I going to post or publish something that will be used against me in a legal matter?
- Can what I post inadvertently do damage to a case or to the firm?
- Is there a risk that what I am posting could be viewed as giving out privileged information?
- Are there potential conflicts of interest by being "friends" or "connections" with judges on social media?
- Can it be a perceived as an endorsement when you have a matter that comes before a judge and you happen to be "friends" with the judge on Facebook or you like their Facebook page?
- How do I avoid posting something in a blog or on social media that could be considered providing legal advice or establishing an attorney-client relationship?
- As a managing partner, how do I control what our attorneys are publishing on social media, as the Internet can be such a "wild, wild west"?

While these are legitimate concerns, the risks are often perceived to be greater than they actually are.[7] Some lawyers who have made mistakes using social media have garnered press attention, yet the numbers of those cases are relatively small.

You likely have heard of cases where prosecutors' and judges' use of social media have led to serious consequences. For example, several years ago , a former prosecutor faced felony charges after allegedly threatening bodily injury to a former employer on Facebook.[8] In another instance, an assistant district attorney supposedly used Facebook to post photos of himself that were deemed to be inappropriate and offensive.[9] The South Carolina Supreme Court reprimanded a recent law school graduate for posting misleading information about both his legal skills and experience on social media.[10] Sending offensive tweets resulted in one deputy attorney general's termination from his job.

Other examples include a criminal defense attorney who was subjected to an ethics complaint after attempting to sway public opinion in a discovery video of an undercover drug buy that was posted on YouTube. Disclosing attorney-client confidence in a blog by using clients' real first names, nicknames, and/or jail identifications resulted in discipline for one assistant public defender. In her blog, she shared not only their names, but also revealed cases, testimony and other privileged, damaging, or embarrassing details. Contempt of court charges were pressed against a county prosecutor in Texas, who subsequently plead guilty for discussing a felony murder case on Facebook, and using Twitter to not only discuss a case, but also linking to documents under court seal, resulted in court charges against a commercial litigator in the state of California.

Most would agree these publicized cases involve lapses of judgment—threatening an employer, indecent exposure, misrepresentation, offensive statements, potential jury tampering, breaching attorney-client confidentiality, distributing documents placed under seal—and all of these actions violated ethical codes via the use of social media. The legal risks are not inherent in the use of social media, but instead are related to lawyers' poor choices.

Lack of knowledge of proper social media usage can also create issues. Perhaps you have heard of the Kentucky judge who was reprimanded for liking the Facebook pages of lawyers and a candidate for judicial office[11]—a move likened to a public endorsement. The ruling raises questions around standard behavior on social media, such as in liking or "following" a person's online profile, and what it actually means.

If you're akin to the judge in this example, who stated he didn't understand what liking a Facebook page meant, you should step back and consider how you would engage with your peers offline. If your association with a lawyer were documented (i.e. a photographer snapping a picture of you and said lawyer at an event), would you attend the event or allow the photo to be taken? If being linked to an individual offline could create conflicts, then you should assume being associated with that individual online could also potentially be problematic. How you ethically conduct yourself in person should guide your decisions about whom you connect with and how you conduct yourself online.

It's understandable that these real-life examples from the legal field can lead to a general distrust of new technologies. Bar associations across the country continue to grapple with the ethics and code of conduct guidelines involving social media and online communication in general, as it is understood that technology is driving this new way of communicating, branding, and marketing. Most involved are clear on the fact that social media is not going away anytime soon, so some guidelines must be put in place. While exact rules are yet to be established, first and foremost, common sense should dictate behavior and decisions with the use of social media and content marketing, just like in the offline world.

With more lawyers and firms creating blogs and seeing success with them as a client attraction and retention tactic, attorneys who want to adopt this strategy often struggle with the best way to use social media for marketing purposes while not violating solicitation and advertising rules, which can vary from state to state around the country.

Consider that lawyers can educate laymen on (1) legal topics, (2) recognizing legal problems, and (3) making intelligent selection of counsel. Many, in fact, do just this via presentations at seminars or conferences. Some lawyers also share articles, press releases about legal wins, and relevant content by others via email newsletters with their clients and interested parties. Providing education by writing a blog, conducting a webinar, and posting links to those on social media profiles is a natural evolution of these more traditional practices. The key here is avoiding the risk of being perceived as establishing a client relationship. You're very likely using certain language in your traditional methods that are appropriate to include here, such as "the focus of what you're sharing is general in nature," or you may include recommendations on obtaining a lawyer and even state that your presentation or response should not be considered legal advice.

If you were speaking at a conference, how would you respond to a question from an audience member about a legal issue that pertains to them? Likely, your response would include the advice to seek legal counsel. Such advice is also appropriate here. You may also avoid the problem altogether by composing your response so it is not specific to their individual legal problem, but rather is applicable to a general scenario.

When implementing content marketing and social media, the content you publish and share should be created using this very approach. Besides written disclaimers about a client relationship and recommendations to obtain a lawyer for legal problems, it's best that your content be written or produced (i.e. video) from an educational perspective, directed toward a general audience. How you frame your advice is important. If you use a client's case as an example, stating that you've obtained written permission from that client is always recommended. And it needn't be said that you should never include false, fraudulent, misleading, deceptive, self-laudatory or unfair statements in your content. Unless you've obtained certification, don't state that you're a specialist. The key here is applying the tried-and-true guidelines about legal advertising in the digital world just as you would elsewhere.

In today's social world, every individual within the law firm is their own brand. Before the advent of the Internet and social media marketing, the law firm was the brand to be represented. Now, every individual is a brand within the context of the law firm. Creating a personal profile on a social network, such as LinkedIn, is a cause for concern for some attorneys who are worried about violating codes of conduct as they fill out their profile. Again, what you say and how you say it is important. The manner in which you provide information about yourself and your practice offline should guide how you state your information online. More information on how to maximize LinkedIn is provided later in this book.

> For Power Tips for your LinkedIn Profile go to www.MicheleRuiz.com/ ContentMarketingResources.

Mitigating risks in the use of social media should be approached in the same manner as you would mitigate any behavioral and communication risks. What is important to understand in all of these scenarios is that just as there are guidelines and rules to cover what you currently communicate via email, phone, and offline, the same guidelines should be adapted for using social media, which is simply another tool used to communicate. Guidance on how to avoid impropriety or the appearance of it is best addressed in policy manuals that govern attorney and staff conduct, as well as social and digital interactions related to the firm and the information the firm allows to be shared. And importantly, these guidelines need to be followed up with training. This is no different than addressing sexual harassment in employee manuals and then conducting trainings to further educate staff on proper behavior.

By nature, the legal industry is cautious. Often, managing partners tend to want to create policies that are far too restrictive because of a lack of understanding about social media, fear about risks, or concern about the amount of resources needed to properly manage and monitor their employees' use of social media. The easy solution for them at that juncture has often been to try to avoid it altogether.

But clamping down in this situation is actually contradictory to the whole purpose of using social media to engage, share, and build trust with your target audience. This is also a detrimental position, as it opens room for competitors who grasp the significance of content marketing and social media to gain market share if you aren't present on the platforms. Additionally, as mentioned earlier, it can influence potential hires to go with another firm that is perceived to be more current and savvy about this new digital world.

Last, imposing overly restrictive policies can create a legal risk by creating an environment where attorneys are not comfortable with online networks. Consider the modern practice environment in which locating and using social media content is becoming ever more important in legal cases.[12] Like in so many other professions, technological skills are frequently desired, if not required. A lawyer who is not knowledgeable with the use of technology including social media and keeping abreast of trends and practices can incur the ramifications of not providing competent representation as several bar associations have pointed out and as addressed in the American Bar Associations summary of its 2014 Fall Meeting *Legal Ethics of Social Media*.[13]

The key here is to follow best practices and useful guidelines on the appropriate way to market and publish information digitally, without violating established regulations and policies, and ultimately bringing on experts to guide you through that process, if necessary.

Fear should not stop you from using the most important communication tool of our age for marketing and building your book of business. In fact, educating laymen about changes in the law and using online networks to promote that education is a powerful way to remind your clients and potential clients of your firm's prowess. In the end, the benefits of social media far outweigh the risks.

4 You are a Brand Within Your Firm

A brand can be anything—a symbol, design, name, sound, reputation, emotion, employees, tone of voice, and much more—that separates one thing from another. Branding applies to everything from your website, to your logo or brochure, to ultimately, the content you put out into the digital space. Each lawyer is a brand within the umbrella brand of his or her firm. Today, branding is becoming important on a personal level because clients often make choices about a law firm based on the perception of or a relationship with an individual attorney.

With social media, you have the opportunity to create a recognizable personal brand. In this context, instead of a logo or a slogan, the story you tell about yourself becomes your brand. Your expertise, your profile photo on LinkedIn, your username or handle on Twitter, your blog's URL, and the reviews about you found online all reveal your brand. However, it's important to be cognizant that your online presence is constantly visible. Whether it is Friday at noon or Sunday morning, there's information on online networks about you and your activity when you aren't in the office. Regardless of where you are—in court or at an event or a family gathering—people form impressions about you without making the distinction between what occurs when you are in the office and who you are during your "off time." They continue to associate you as the lawyer from XYZ law firm. When you understand this crucial fact, it will influence what content you publish and the words and images you choose to share, even on a personal level.

If you have a purposeful marketing strategy in the world of social media, you can create a powerful and influential personal brand. It can attract potential clients who otherwise may not otherwise know about you. Many clients make a decision about retaining a law firm based on one particular lawyer's profile or information. Everything from your blog, LinkedIn profile, to your Facebook posts and Tweets helps to create your personal brand and influence potential clients to reach out to you.

A client's impression of you is based on the information and thoughts you've shared in the digital space. If you have failed to supply any information, i.e. you have a LinkedIn profile with sparse information about yourself or your strengths, the client searching for a particular need will likely gloss right over you and move on to the lawyer or firm that is doing a better job of selling themselves and their expertise online. Here's the key: You are what you publish, so publish enough and publish appropriately.

Growing Your Value Through Personal Branding and Thought Leadership

Personal branding within the firm is more than simply creating a name for yourself. If you are in a more traditional firm and on the partner track, in most cases, becoming a partner will be predicated on your ability to show your value and bring in business. Another way is by bringing recognition to the firm. Leveraging social media can be a great tactic to support these career goals.

Numerous lawyers do this today in every niche, ranging from real estate, tax, criminal, and family law to estate planning, and they are using strategies online. There are many ways to approach this, such as having a well-written profile on social platforms like LinkedIn and your Facebook business page, using Twitter and blogging, and sharing relevant information such as articles, consistently on social media, which in turn builds your network. Other ways include creating video blogs and publishing them on YouTube, sharing PowerPoint presentations on LinkedIn, and using other similar platforms like SlideShare, video recording speaking opportunities and sharing those recordings on social networks, and publishing white papers or eBooks that educate about legal topics that are relevant to your target clients and distributing them online.

As mentioned before, these strategies often lead to opportunities to be included in media coverage that positions you as a thought leader or subject matter expert, attracting recognition and clients to your firm. There are instances of lawyers who have crossed over the $1,000-plus per hour threshold once they've become well established as an expert in a particular field of law.[14] These high billing rates are supported by the online reputation and strength of the brand a lawyer is able to build within his or her niche. Having been in broadcast journalism for over 18 years, my experience has been that the legal experts brought in to assist in providing an insightful perspective on various cases and subjects were all perceived to be subject matter experts, established as such through content publishing and reputation within the industry, and personal relationships with journalists.

If this seems overwhelming and you're not sure how to begin, don't worry. All of this and more is covered in the Part II in this book.

Can I Have Someone Do This for Me?

In an environment that is driven by hourly billing, it's not surprising that attorneys may consider having others do all of their social media marketing. When I'm asked, "Can I have someone do this for me?," my response is more often than not, "for certain aspects of your strategy and content, yes" If you want to achieve all of the goals talked about in this book, you need to have some significant involvement in the strategy and content.

Here's why: The magic of social media is your unique voice, tone, and personality shining through your content. When a separate individual is hired to write or create the content for you, it becomes less personal and thus less engaging. A blog in your own voice is much more telling of your talents and strengths than a more vanilla content piece that offers generalized information found in numerous places on the web. Much of the benefit derived from content marketing and social media comes from building a relationship with the audience or targeted client. That relationship is built when the user learns about you and gets a feel for how you speak, the words you use, etc.

This is not to say that you can't have assistance (internally with staff, or externally with content experts or content creators) with developing the strategy, scheduling your postings, or monitoring the online conversations as well as content creation once a strategy and process is set in place. The key is that you are involved to the degree necessary to make sure it represents the essence of who you are as a person and an attorney.

Whomever you choose to support you in these efforts represents you and your personal brand. The question is who has the best skill set and credentials to help your content stand out in a world saturated with content? Often, lawyers hire marketing experts. I believe the best are content experts. The same type of experts corporations bring in. They call their content strategies "corporate journalism". In fact, the 2014 State of Digital and Content Marketing Survey by the Zeughauser Group, Greentarget, and the American Lawyer recommends firms embrace the principles of corporate journalism. They define it as "a practice that combines an organization's market intelligence and subject matter expertise with the credibility and narrative techniques of professional journalism". The report further points out:

"Done well, corporate journalism should incorporate elements of traditional journalism, including:

- Journalistic commitment to accuracy, fairness and credibility
- The critical notion that journalism serves its audience above
- all others
- Direct, succinct, lively writing that favors plain English over industry jargon"

Many corporations bring in journalists and communication companies such as mine headed by former journalists because we know how to craft compelling stories so their content rises above the online noise, and ultimately helps achieve their business objectives. Beyond compelling content creation skills, it's ideal that they have social media marketing expertise as well as a deep understanding of your business objectives.

Typically, the ideal individual for this work will NOT be the firm's intern who happens to know how to use social media tools. It's surprising how often interns become the designated social media point people. I often have said, "Would you let an intern write your human resources policy and distribute it? If not, then why would you hand over your most important communication tool, content and strategy to that inexperienced person?" I share more about this and further techniques to create content in time-efficient ways in the chapter *Impactful Content Creation and Distribution Strategies* to help you.

How Much Time is This Going to Take?

Initially, it will take time to develop a successful social business strategy. You will need to be clear about your goals, how you will measure success, what type of content you want to create, and how frequently you are going to engage on the various platforms. Once you have your strategy set in place, it may take some time to determine which social platforms and what types of content work best for you and learn how to use them effectively. At the beginning, it may take a bit longer to create your first pieces of content, as well.

So here's the deal: you will invest more time upfront, as you would with any important career objective. But once you get comfortable with your strategy and gain a clear understanding of your objectives, you can develop a strategy and process that likely will take less of your time than more traditional ways of marketing your firm. If you consider that you're "marketing" while you're sleeping in on a Saturday morning because people are finding your content online, you can see the return on your investment (ROI) can be even greater. In some instances, the efforts become seamless and with a minimal daily investment, the engine of your social media marketing can keep humming. I give you more guidance on this in the chapter "Pulling a Content Marketing Strategy Together." I also offer other resources for lawyers to help speed up the learning curve so you accomplish your goals faster.

> For more resources and guidance go to www.MicheleRuiz.com/
> ContentMarketingResources.

Attorneys frequently make the mistake of thinking they can just jump in with a social media profile and expect to see positive results. They often quickly get frustrated and abandon their efforts when the results don't prove as immediately fruitful as they anticipated. Social media involvement without a set plan is like simply playing around on Facebook—and that's not why you bought this book. You want to see results and achieve your career goals. Just as it takes time to build meaningful relationships in the offline world, it takes time to grow your network and build trust online. Remember, the Client Acquisition funnel covered in the Chapter 3 and the steps it takes to get potential clients to contact you or others to refer you to their own network can often take time. But it is well worth the investment, as many other attorneys have discovered.

How Do I Get Support and Buy-in from the Firm?

While more and more law firms are recognizing the value of social media marketing as a business priority, there are still many that do not have a strategy. Some also maintain very restrictive policies for their attorneys and staff, as referenced in Chapter 3 in the section, "But Aren't Their Legal Risks to Using Social Media." A better position to be in would be to have the top management of your firm not only support but also embrace a social business philosophy and make it a priority as part of the business development roadmap. In this latter scenario, individual lawyers are set up for success in their use of social media and content marketing.

However, if you work for a firm that has no direct social media policy, this shouldn't hinder your progress in using these powerful tools. You can certainly set up your social profiles to be geared toward your own career objectives and publish and share content under your own name if your firm allows for that. You might also set up a website under your own name and publish a blog that is related to your subject matter expertise. In your bio area, you might include that you are a lawyer at XYZ law firm, so there remains an association that you are still a brand within the umbrella brand of the firm. This is particularly useful if you want to leverage the firm's brand equity.

You can also look into publishing a white paper or a SlideShare, again using those pieces of content to build your reputation as a thought leader, increasing your credibility and furthering your reputation as a subject matter expert. Once it becomes evident to the decision makers in your firm that you have implemented successful strategies to share your content through social media, you can possibly persuade them to be more open minded about embracing digital strategies. Since fear is typically the number one reason managing partners try to control or limit social media usage, you might find it helpful to share the points made in the earlier chapter "But Aren't Their Legal Risks to Using Social Media" as well as refer to the *2014 State of Digital and Content Marketing Survey by the Zeughauser Group, Greentarget, and the American Lawyer*. The American Bar Associations summary of its 2014 Fall Meeting Legal Ethics of Social Media could also be helpful to make your case.

You might also consider sharing data about what is happening currently in the legal industry regarding the use of digital technologies. A study conducted by the ABA called *The 2014 Legal Technology Survey* highlights important information about trends in the industry concerning web and communication technologies, social networks, and the growing importance of these in everyday practice.

Another common objection is "we don't really need to use social media as we have a great reputation in place already." Understanding the ocean of opportunity that social media brings to business development efforts requires some understanding of the tools and why they work. If the leaders at your firm do not have that understanding, it is important to convey that opting to not participate is not the best response to this new media revolution, as your competition is certainly not sitting on the sidelines. Participating in a thoughtful and strategic way as described here can give your firm's management team the confidence that you are approaching it with the firm's best interest in mind and help them view your efforts as a true asset that you bring to the table.

Some firm leaders are comfortable in believing that traditional legal marketing works just fine. As mentioned earlier, traditional methods do have their place within the overall efforts of the firm to gain new clients. However, it is clear that these methods are often more costly and are not always the ideal investment of your most precious resource, your time. There will be far greater benefits and a stronger reach to your potential clients through the introduction of new media and digital platforms, and including them with a healthy mix of the more traditional methods that your firm is accustomed to deploying.

While the firm already has an established reputation, the technological advancements with smartphones combined with the evolution of social media make it important to be mindful that a paradigm shift has occurred. People expect to engage with a more approachable brand in today's connected environment, and that includes the firm's overall brand. People of all ages are growing accustomed to being part of the conversation and having a dialogue with the brands and products or services they engage with, rather than being fed information on a one-way basis, as is the case with more traditional marketing efforts. Social media is a more personalized way of connecting and building relationships with potential clients—and your potential clients have come to expect that as the norm.

In an already busy schedule, concerns about the availability of time to implement a proper strategy is often another barrier to beginning at all. Learning social media marketing begins, like any other new skill, one step at a time. With the right strategy, it can take less time than traditional marketing efforts and produce greater results. This book goes into detail about how to do just that in Part II.

Of course, you can always gift wrap a copy of this book and share it with the powers that be who need persuading in your firm. ☺

With the right information, you can make a large difference at your firm. Recently, a young lawyer came to me for advice. The managing partners of his firm simply did not think engaging in social media marketing was necessary. But this particular lawyer happens to embrace and use social media quite well. Once he demonstrated the value of creating strong and engaging content in order to build his reputation, as well as the reputation of his firm, he was able to convince the partners to support his efforts and ultimately proved instrumental in changing his firm's culture.

Who Ultimately Owns Your Content and Your Social Media?

The issue of digital content ownership has been debated for some time now and is, in fact, the genesis of certain court cases. For instance, questions about who owns an individual's Twitter followers, especially if they are significant to the employer's business objectives, have been brought up in court. If a Twitter following was built on company time or through using company resources, even though a personal account, there are differing opinions about who in fact owns the results of an individual's social media marketing efforts. Employment lawyer Renee Jackson addressed this in an interview she gave to Forbes.[15]

> *Twitter followers, Facebook fans, and LinkedIn connections are customers, potential customers, or other valuable contacts, and gaining a direct line of communication to these people is the point of using social media in the first place. The time and money spent growing a following, promoting a brand, developing an industry niche or expertise, and sharing content is invaluable and cannot be recouped easily. The line between a personal and professional social media account can be blurry, so if this ownership issue is not hashed out at the beginning of employment, the employer and the employee may both believe the account is theirs. As you can imagine, litigation arises out of this grey area. However, we do know that courts may consider the following factors when determining ownership of social media accounts: who set up the accounts and directed the content, when the accounts were set up (during or before employment), who had access to the accounts and passwords, whether and how the handle or account was associated with the employer's name or brand, and the value of the followers, fans, or connections.*

There remain many open-ended questions around social media marketing in practice. That said, it is important to gain a clear understanding with your firm on guidelines, if they exist. This should include the ownership of your content. From the onset, there should be no questions about who owns the content or your accounts on social media platforms should your relationship with your firm change.

Additionally, you should know that some platforms still attempt to find ways to leverage a user's content for their own purposes and potential monetary gain. Instagram had just such an issue when attempting to change privacy policies, allowing the company to use individuals' images and content without their explicit consent. It was not long before Instagram chose to change their path, given the huge outcry from their users. However, this is a continually evolving area of the digital environment, so be clear that you must keep your eyes and ears open as you delve in. If this area concerns you, one solution is to host all of your content on your own website or blog, and then link to it through your social platforms, thus clearly delineating the ownership of the content.

Part 2
The How-To

So far, we've discussed why social media and content marketing needs to be an integral part of your business development strategy. Now we are at the point where we really get down to brass tacks and delve into how to implement your strategy effectively. You will learn exact methods and tactics you can employ on a regular basis in order to leverage social media as a powerful communication and client acquisition tool.

In Part II, you will find information, answers, and guidance on the following:

- What you'll need to get started in implementing a compelling and successful content marketing strategy
- What decisions you need to make before you commit to a strategy
- An explanation of the major social media platforms to better understand what they are about and decide which are best suited for your strategy
- A step-by-step process to develop an effective strategy that brings the results you want
- A usable definition of "content" and an understanding of which of the various types of content available can be the most impactful for your legal practice
- The ins and outs of creating content that your would-be clients will find valuable and want to share with their own networks, ultimately driving new clients to you
- Ways to make the content for your website, blog posts, and social media more exciting, engaging, and interesting, using the same compelling storytelling skills journalists use every day
- What to do with all that great content once you've created it, including where to distribute it and how to make sure your clients and potential clients are actually seeing your content
- How to become a thought leader and the "go-to" expert
- Top mistakes for lawyers to avoid

Often, one of the hardest steps in getting started is deciding what types of content to produce and what the content should be about. To help with this process, I have provided content ideas to get you started on the website. There, you'll find templates and other tools that will set you up for success from the onset.

For content ideas go to www.MicheleRuiz.com/ContentMarketing Resources .

5   What You Need to Know Before You Start a Content Marketing Strategy

Before you get started on your strategy, it is important to ask yourself some key questions.

Why are you thinking of using social media?

If you are simply following the "trend" because everyone else is doing it, or you haven't yet thought about measureable results that you'd like to achieve, you'll likely be spending a lot of time doing busy work while not seeing results that reflect in your firm's bottom line.

How exactly will you define and measure success?

If you've established no measureable goals, you won't be able to define success. If you can't analyze the results of your efforts, you won't be able to feel confident that the efforts you're expending are fruitful and leading to more client business. It takes time to see results. You should be prepared that it could take a year or longer before you can make the connection between your efforts and your client acquisition results. Patience here is key.

Who is going to be responsible for the social media efforts?

Someone needs to lead the strategy. Will this be you or someone else? While more than one person can handle the execution, it's best to have one person responsible for the overall strategy and outcomes. Actively interacting and communicating on social media platforms is an important part of an effective plan and strategy and should not be left to chance or random support.

Who is going to be responsible for communicating on your behalf, responding to people's comments and questions about your postings, and even possible complaints related to you or your practice?

While tempting, an intern is not best suited to this work simply because "they're young and know social media." That type of thinking is a big mistake. The person who manages the social profiles should be experienced enough in your business to understand your business objectives, as well as have the maturity to write communications appropriately on your behalf. You should be able to trust their decision-making abilities and judgment. That's not to say entry-level staffers can't assist with efforts. The key is that there should be real-time supervision and proper management.

Have you considered your resources?

Are you a sole practitioner? If so, it's you or you and an assistant who will likely be managing your marketing and social media. Or are you part of a larger firm, with a dedicated marketing team that can help your efforts? Do you have partners in the same practice group and can implement a strategy in which all the lawyers in the practice group are involved in creating and sharing content?

In any of these scenarios, resources and time are critically important in developing a successful strategy that is consistent, of high quality, and brings you more clients. You also will need to consider your editorial calendar, as is covered in the chapter "Pulling a Content Marketing Strategy Together." Having a plan that addresses who will manage the content distribution and posting schedule as laid out in your calendar will be an important step, as well as creating a plan for the overall implementation of your strategy in order to gain the positive results you want.

How will you promote your social media presence when you launch?

Hoping your social presences grow organically and that Facebook content and page will be found by your target audience is not likely a plan that will lead to meaningful business results. As we've seen happen with Facebook (and others will likely follow suit, as well), you'll need to promote your social media profiles. The platforms' algorithms will limit who sees your content and pages unless you pay to advertise or promote your activity and posts. Will you add icons and calls to action on your website or within your email signature? If you send out newsletters, you'll also want to promote your social media profiles within them. Will you use some traditional paid advertising? Launching without a plan on how your target clients will find you on social media can be a time waster.

If you're part of a firm and not a sole practitioner, there are some additional factors to consider when getting started. When you are creating and pushing out content via social media even under your own name, you still represent your firm. Some law firms embrace social media and content marketing. Some of these firms' websites may, in fact, have a blog associated with the firm. Some even encourage their lawyers to create content such as blog posts under their own name and have a publishing system established under the firm's brand. They may also have marketing managers to assist in this process.

Other firms may simply have a social media presence, such as a Twitter account or a Facebook page, but have not implemented a firm-wide strategy that involves many, if not all, of its lawyers. Last, there are those law firms who are not doing anything notable on social media at all.

Depending on your firm's level of social media usage and the culture of the firm and its managing partners, there are certain steps I recommend you take to get underway. If you are part of a firm that has an active social media presence and blog under the firm's name, or has some social presence but no content strategy, you might want to explore the following:

- If you were to publish a blog, video blogs, or other content, would the firm host it on their own blogging platforms, YouTube channel (for video blogs), etc.? If so, there is no need to set up your own blog website. However, having said this, if you're concerned that there would be a question as to who would retain ownership of your content if you were to leave the firm, you may elect to have your own blog website.
- If there is a marketing manager in place at your firm, would he or she be willing to offer any assistance as you create the content?

The key is involving the individuals at your firm who are focused on marketing into the process of your content creation. This can help provide assurances to the powers that be that you are cognizant of protecting the integrity of your law firm's brand, while at the same time creating compelling content to grow your personal brand.

- Also, investigating specifics in regard to the firm's marketing goals may be a worthwhile expenditure of your time. Incorporating these goals into your thought process is important, so as you are sharing content, and your efforts align with the firm's goals, the firm can recognize this fact. This can, in turn, lead to more support within your firm for your social marketing efforts. For example, if your firm has a goal to expand its footprint in Texas, and you create a blog or other content that showcases your area of expertise that happens to mention an example that came up in Texas, your blog can be seen as aligning your effort with the firm's, and ultimately your efforts being in the firm's best interest, as well.

- Would the firm be willing to promote your blog posts and content in the same manner in which they are promoting other firm content, regardless if it's hosted on the firm's platform or your own website? Doing so would help the firm by showcasing the expertise it has on staff, as well as providing the firm with additional fresh content. It's a win-win for both you and the firm.

- If you will not be using the firm's platforms to host your content, then when setting up your own blog website under your name, you need to be clear on what guidelines, if any, there are around using the firm's name and logo within your content. This is especially important if the firm is well recognized and you would like to leverage your firm's brand equity. This would come into play, for instance, in your bio area on the various platforms or the "about me" section on your blog and blog posts.

- You will want to discuss in some detail your social media efforts with your managing partners at your law firm. Some firms may require approval, while others may not. Similarly, some are sophisticated and actually have a social media policy in place that you can refer to, yet many will not and it's best to get clarity as you move forward in order to be sure you are working within their guidelines.

In the event you are at a firm that is not committed to social media marketing and you are doing it on your own, it's good to remember you still represent your firm's brand in everything you do online. Here are some further guidelines:

- I suggest you to talk about your social media efforts with key people at the law firm.
- Knowing the firm's marketing goals will also still be worthwhile. As mentioned in the first example, this is important when you are sharing content. If what you're doing aligns with the firm's goals, it can lead to more support for your efforts.

If you're unfortunately part of a firm that actually discourages using social media, it may help to refer back to Chapter 4 about getting buy-in at your firm in order to help overcome these obstacles.

Last, if you're a sole practitioner, then luckily you determine all the rules you're going to abide by through this process. Now that you've evaluated the landscape that you're operating in, the next step is to get clear on who your ideal clients are.

Targeting Your Ideal Client

"Seeing results could take time. Most people want to jump right in and launch multiple channels at once and simply worry about the strategy later." – Kevin O'Keefe, Legal Blogger[16]

It is very important to understand that having a strategy for your content marketing is akin to having a map on a road trip. You wouldn't likely go on a trip across country without a navigation system to guide your way. Similarly, you need a plan for how you will approach your content marketing.

One key element is to know your clients well, and that means identifying the attributes of your "ideal" client. These attributes are used to create what is known as a "client persona" or a detailed description of that ideal client for you or your firm. They are also referred to as your primary audience or persona 1. In creating this persona, think about that ideal client as if they were sitting across the table from you at lunch.

- Are they existing clients?
- Potential clients using other law firms?
- Potential new clients without an existing legal relationship?
- Where are they located geographically?
- What are their key demographics:

  o Gender
  o Marital status (if relevant)
  o Sexual Orientation (if relevant)
  o Type of business/career
  o Role/position in their company
  o Age
  o Education
  o Ethnicity (if relevant)
  o Primary language
  o Health status/disabilities (if relevant)
  o Home ownership (if relevant)
  o Values – religious and cultural (if relevant)
  o Hobbies (if relevant)
  o What do they do for leisure? (if relevant)

- What are their needs?
- What are their goals or what is important to them?
- What keeps them up at night or causes them stress?
- What issue should they be aware of or what should they know to prevent problems?

- Is cost of legal fees important to them?
- How are you best able to help them?
- What do they need to believe about you and/or your firm?
- When and where do they find their information online?
- What action do you want them to take? Sign up for your newsletter, webinar, contact you, make a referral, etc?

Knowing these nuances helps to nail down your messaging, decide the content that you create, and fine tune your strategy to be relevant to your ideal client. With our clients, we even give their target persona's names, because if done thoroughly, you know so much about them that you can think of them as a real person.

During the process of creating your client personas, the other person to define is the individual that can influence your potential clients to take action, or persona 2. These influencers are nearly as important as your main audience, given the fact that they can send clients your way. For example, in estate planning, an influencer can be a financial planner, who can opine about your services, the value you bring to the financial planning process, and give you a positive referral.

In order for your strategy to be effective, it needs to address each one—the target/primary client and his or her influencers. The key is to detail enough information that the target client or influencer connects intuitively and says to himself, "yes, that's me" or feels "this attorney is speaking to me."

Note that you can have more than one primary target client and more than one influencer for each one. There is a Client Persona Template on my website to help you with this process.

> For more resources and guidance go to www.MicheleRuiz.com/
> ContentMarketingResources.

One of the most successful examples of expending the effort to get clear on who you are speaking to, how to be relevant, and how to connect with on a personal level is from the Obama campaign.

Barack Obama was the first presidential candidate to fully embrace social media and content marketing (blogs, videos, images, infographics) geared to target voters and their influencers even before he declared his candidacy. Many experts believe his online strategy was a significant factor in his winning the presidential campaign.

Setting Goals Up Front

Just as you would any marketing effort, it is important that you define your business goals and set up your social media strategy to support those goals, keeping in mind what equates to success for you and your firm. Once you can articulate specifically the types of clients you want to attract to build your book of business, then the next step is to think about your objectives. How do you measure success in this seemingly amorphous environment? You evaluate success based on your objectives, each of which should be tangible and measurable. Think about what you want to gain for your career and your firm through your social media investment, and create goals for as many of these objectives as you are able.

For example, your goals might include results such as "increase the number of divorce cases I bring in by 10% in the next 12 months from the Los Angeles area," or to increase the amount of work you're doing with a current client. Another objective might be "bring in the litigation work from XYZ client that is currently being handled by ABC law firm by the end of 2016", or "increase revenues from clients doing business in China by 23% in the next 18 months." All are good examples of tangible goals against which your efforts can be measured.

Another set of business objectives might be related to thought leadership goals. For example, "be included in media articles, reports, and other publications as an expert for personal tax matters in the Tristate area starting in four months" could be an objective.

Here are a few other examples of what you might consider successful results:

- Increased client acquisition by 15%
- Greater number of client leads over the last year
- Increased referral business by 5%
- Increased revenue by a targeted amount

The key is that any goal you establish needs to be measurable. This is how you'll be able to evaluate if what you're doing is getting game-changing results. You may have heard of "Smart Goals," which means goals that are specific, measurable, attainable, realistic and timely (within a time frame). This concept is fundamental to an efficient and successful strategy. You're not ready to launch an effective social media marketing strategy if your desired outcomes are nebulous goals, such as "I want to get more business," "I want to grow my social media following," or "I want to use social media because everyone else is doing it."

This is an area where attorneys often fail at their efforts. Not defining success in measurable ways means you can't justify the amount of effort you're putting into your social media and you can't tell if the results are worthwhile.

In fact, people often abandon social media marketing efforts because they don't set out with specific tangible objectives. Therefore, when they dive in, spending time and financial resources on social media, they can't see the ROI of their efforts. It's like trying to drive from California to New York without a GPS. In other words, it can be frustrating.

Taking the time to measure the effectiveness of your strategy as you learn what is successful and what isn't, and using those results to optimize and focus your efforts in the areas where you get the most return, is one of the success secrets for this process.

Success through your efforts can be defined quite differently for firms and individuals, so before you are able to measure the effectiveness of your efforts, you must define your own goals clearly. What are the types of actions you want your followers or clients to take, or what effects do you want to see from your social media strategies that most directly improve your business and increase your and your firm's success?

It's important to note that we are talking about business goals here, and not about social media objectives just yet. Ideally, a strategic social plan will support achieving both your business objectives and the more specific social media objectives. More specifics on this can be found in Chapter 10.

To download the Business Objectives Template go to www.MicheleRuiz. com/ContentMarketingResources

Client-Attracting Value Propositions

For the most part, clients have many options for legal services. As a result, it can be challenging for lawyers to bring in new clients or even retain current clients in a competitive environment. This has become even more difficult in recent years due to a weak economy and many potential clients being very cost conscious and sensitive to perceived pricey legal fees. On top of that, online legal solutions such as LegalZoom and Rocket Lawyer have created an expectation that there may not be a need to consult with an attorney at all and that one can handle certain matters themselves.

So how does an attorney stand out from the myriad of options? This is where a strong value proposition comes into play. A value proposition is a clear statement of the tangible results a client will receive from using your services. It focuses on the business value of your offering. Once you've developed your unique value proposition, I recommend you incorporate it into your social media, such as in the description section of your LinkedIn profile, the tagline of your blog, in your Power-Point presentations that will be shared on your social media, and other related content.

Some lawyers say something like, "I'm an attorney. I do corporate tax work." BORING! Clients, like most people, are thinking, "So what? Why should I waste my valuable time talking to you?" Or, if they have an attorney at the time, "I already have a lawyer. Why should I make a change?"

Here's an example of how an effective value proposition can drive business from the automotive industry: Volvo as a brand doesn't sell cars. It sells safety. Consumers have many options in buying a car. According to a 2014 study done by *Consumer Reports* about brand perception, Volvo has long hung its hat on safety, and this focus continues to define their brand and pay off today.[17] In the minds of consumers, there is a single, clear choice when it comes to safety. In other words, consumers buy a Volvo over other cars because they believe in the company's value proposition – its cars are among the most reliable and safest options on the market.

To develop your value proposition, think about what's important to your current and potential clients and the value you bring to the table in regard to those issues. This value proposition is not about your legal services. It is about the impact of what you do. A strong value proposition is specific, tangible, and often uses numbers, percentages, or results. For example:

In the past five years alone, our firm has collected over $100 million in settlements and judgments for our clients.

Some lawyers find it difficult to quantify the measurable results clients realize from using their services. It might seem insurmountable to relay a strong value proposition when one cannot put into tangible results the value they bring to their clients. Rather than struggling to put into words a rather intangible or abstract benefit that the client will gain by engaging you as an attorney, try to get the idea across through creative and compelling storytelling. Give specific examples of cases in which you've been able to add these more abstract values. Potential clients will garner your capabilities and strengths from the stories.

Here are a few more examples of client-attracting value proposition:

We help large companies reduce the number of employee workplace claims. In a litigious environment, this is a critical issue for most businesses. One of our recent clients, a large logistics company with 130 employees, was struggling with reducing costs related to these types of claims. We helped them decrease the number of claims by 68% in the last 3 years, while growing the number of employees at the same time.

I help entrepreneurs save time, money, and aggravation as they navigate the complexities of trademark registration and trademark litigation. I also help them avoid costly legal mistakes in the selection and use of their trademarks. One of my recent clients was launching a new software solution and thought they could go to market with a certain product name. After my firm did a review of the trademark search, we discovered that another company was using that name for a similar offering. This meant that my client could have been sued for trademark infringement. Being sued for trademark infringement can be devastating to a new venture. They hence decided to use a different name.

Another way to think about a value proposition is to think in terms of opportunity cost. Opportunity cost relates to opportunities that are lost to your client because of the method in which they are currently operating. This can also be defined as business goals they can't pursue because they are dealing with a problem – both in terms of bandwidth and capital. For example, what could your client be doing with the $75,000 they would not spend in fighting a lawsuit that your services or firm might have prevented?

Strong value propositions are always stated in business terms, and they are tangible and specific. Clients are particularly attracted to phrases that start with words such as:

- Increase
- Decrease
- Faster
- Avoid
- Improve
- Reduce
- Save
- Minimize
- Maximize

Can your expertise provide benefits that start with any of the above words? Remember what your clients care about most – results. What credentials, testimonials, or analysis can you present that give your potential clients a "reason to believe" you are THE lawyer to go to? Further, if you can, extend the "benefits" into actual numbers, which becomes an even more powerful value proposition. Remember, a value proposition is a clear statement of the tangible results clients get from using your legal services. It's focused on the outcomes and the business value of your offering, not on how you do what you do.

Many lawyers in the market are not employing value propositions in their marketing and communication materials or content. By going through this exercise and using a client-attracting value proposition, you will start to differentiate yourself from the competition. I have created a Client-Attraction Value Proposition Worksheet to help you develop your own value proposition.

> To download the Client-Attraction Value Proposition Worksheet go to www.MicheleRuiz.com/ContentMarketingResources.

Now that you're clear on your business objectives and have spent time understanding your ideal clients and the value you provide to them, you're in good shape to develop your social media and content marketing strategy. So let's get started.

6 Social Media: The Basics

With many social networking sites globally, and even more appearing and disappearing daily, it can be daunting not only to figure out how each one works, but also which are best in order to achieve your business goals. When crafting your social media and content marketing strategy, some of the factors to consider are:

- Which social media platforms are your target and current clients most using? Based on your knowledge of your current client base and your practice's "client persona," which of these platforms is the best investment of your time?
  - You don't have to be active on each popular social media platform, so decide which ones you want to invest in. Not all platforms are going to be appropriate for your audience, but by following the steps we've discussed, you can make informed decisions as to which of them is right for your particular situation.

- What resources, and how much time do you truly have to dedicate to this process?
  - Success will not be based on how many platforms you're using. In fact, diving in and trying to do it all, and do each well is setting yourself up to fail and not realizing your business goals. Each platform takes a specific strategy, which is why evaluating your resources and bandwidth is important.

In order to help you know the best way to promote your law firm via social media, we've covered the basics here on the social media platforms most widely used today in building relationships that can lead to revenue growth. We discuss below what each platform is and what kind of audience you can expect to find there.

In addition to helping you choose the appropriate web properties for your needs, you will also learn the steps required to set up your profile in order to maximize each platform. Since the social media companies change the way their platforms work very frequently, I have also offered this step-by-step process in guides available on my website. These guides will be updated as any of the rules or methods change.

> For more resources and guidance go to www.MicheleRuiz.com/
> ContentMarketingResources.

LinkedIn

According to the ABA 2014 TechReport, LinkedIn is the most used social networking site by lawyers.[18] It is also the most under-used social media platform primarily because most lawyers have set up a profile but are not using it for marketing and networking. LinkedIn is particularly well suited to you as an attorney as it is based upon connections, recommendations, and "word-of-mouth" amongst professionals. Through LinkedIn, you can keep up with industry trends, recruit for your law firm, find other lawyers with which to collaborate, provide information on your firm, and attract clients. You'll be able to frame your academic background, your career highlights, your in-depth subject knowledge, your pro bono or other interests, and give a strong sense of who you are as a professional to other LinkedIn members.

LinkedIn is also well known as a job-hunter's search engine, with individuals using the many networks and company profiles to connect with new opportunities. Some attorneys also use the platform to promote their events, ask questions of peers, and discuss legal issues. It is the premier networking and social site for professionals, boasting a whopping 400 million members, with a demographic that tends to be educated, affluent, and influential. In fact, most LinkedIn users have a household income of $75,000 or more.[19]

LinkedIn is as important a platform for business-to-business (B2B) relationships as it is for business-to-consumer (B2C). It is a rich environment to engage with and influence your target audiences, whether they work at large companies or are individuals, such as doctors in private practice. It has changed the paradigm of B2B and B2C marketing to human-to-human (H2H) relationship building.

Remember, the client-acquisition funnel discussed in Chapter 4? Potential clients learn about you, they choose to get information from you, they trust you, and then when they have a need, or know someone who does, they will seek your services. In a nutshell, it is a very effective platform to build your personal brand, establish business relationships with potential clients and influencers, and then build on those relationships in order to generate business.

With its recently launched publishing platform, you can now publish blogs directly on LinkedIn and people can select to follow your postings. LinkedIn calls it the "definitive professional publishing platform" giving members a way to build their professional brand by having a place to post original content. That content, which can be blogs, links to articles, images, quotes, a PowerPoint presentation and more, becomes part of your LinkedIn profile and helps to showcase your expertise.

Not all law firms give LinkedIn its due attention, and those not using it are at risk of losing market share. Consider that LinkedIn as a platform generates more traffic to corporate sites than all of the other social platforms combined, as noted in an Investis IQ Audience Insight Report[20].

These statistics make it clear that LinkedIn is THE lawyer's social network. Many see the platform as a valuable and trusted resource when researching a company or its employees or partners. Because of this, LinkedIn is used as a "calling card" of types, with many adding a link to their LinkedIn profile in their email signatures or using it as a place to send someone who is seeking more information about them as a professional. Search engines also have conditioned the end user that LinkedIn can be trusted, listing the pages in the top results when a searcher is looking for information on a professional.

One of the most valuable facets of LinkedIn is that within the networking arena, you are able to quickly see who and what companies your peers are connected to and request referrals and connections from them to these potentially interesting leads. In other words, you can ask to be introduced to people they know who may be or have valuable contacts for you in your business development efforts.

I strongly recommend setting up a firm profile, known as a company profile, as well as creating your own optimized and fully fleshed out personal profile as an individual attorney. Each attorney at your firm should be connected to the firm's LinkedIn profile. This is important because users are likely to click on the firm profile link and then hopefully form a favorable opinion about you and your practice based on the content and the list of employees at your firm. This, in turn, creates multiple ways for people to land on information about you.

Another benefit of LinkedIn company profiles is that they allow users to follow your firm and keep up with the information and insights pushed out on your company's profile page. As an example, if your firm specializes in patent law, those interested in either your firm specifically or information about this specialty can choose to follow your company page and have access to blogs or PowerPoint presentations that are being shared by your firm's attorneys.

If you've been practicing law for a while, you'll recall the usage of Martindale-Hubbell profiles in order to drive people to a firm and its lawyers. LinkedIn is the modern-day version of this type of leads and traffic engine and, therefore, not a platform to pass over or take lightly. Not only is it tremendously more effective than those more traditional methods, it is also free.

LinkedIn Groups is another unique offering on the LinkedIn platform. It is the perfect online environment in which to attract clients. It is one of the largest forums for professionals on the web, where individuals are able to interact and discuss topics of mutual interest. There are subject-specific groups on the LinkedIn platform around almost any topic.

Let's say you specialize in advertising, promotions, and intellectual property and your target clients are advertising firms. You can easily join a group or groups comprised of individuals in the advertising field in order to attract more clients. Also, think about getting quality referrals. If CPAs are good referrers for your practice, then join a LinkedIn group to connect with CPAs on a regular basis. Or perhaps many of your clients come from trade associations. If so, join a group that is like a trade association, which can be advantageous.

In all these examples, you will benefit from the ability to share content and information with the group that positions you as an expert. This is how you can interact directly with a very targeted group of people to meet your business objectives. Think of it like a networking event, except in this case, held online, 24/7.

Can't find the right group? Then one option is to create a group of your own in order to connect with a specific audience. Let's say your clients and decision makers are general counsels at large companies in the energy sector. You could form a LinkedIn group specifically for general counsels to provide a valuable environment where they can learn, share, and engage with others in this area of focus.

You would host and manage the group yourself by facilitating online discussions and by sharing information, trends, and articles. You could allow others in the group to share educational content, as well. The secondary benefit is that it provides a way to connect with other lawyers who are experts in this field. As a manager of the group, you can more readily be seen as a thought leader in this topic. Being seen as a thought leader in your niche is a strong tactic to add to your strategy, and LinkedIn can be hugely powerful in helping you be perceived as a subject matter expert.

I provide ideas on how to use LinkedIn as part of your content marketing and social media strategy in the next chapter. You can also get my Power Tips for Your LinkedIn profile on my website.

> To access the Power Tips for Your LinkedIn Profile go to www. MicheleRuiz.com/ContentMarketingResources.

Twitter

"In this day and age when technology and social communication is part of the fabric of our personal and business lives, it seems a dereliction of duty for a managing partner to ignore Twitter."
Kevin O'Keefe, Lawyer and Legal Blogger, LexBlog Inc[21]

Twitter is a different kind of social network where you post and read short 140-character messages called tweets. As of this writing, the character limit may change as news has broken about Twitter considering dropping the 140-character length restriction. So look for changes. However, they won't alter the nature of what Twitter has been since its inception – a social network with a real-time focus. And it has become an increasingly important platform for legal experts.

Via this network, you share information and it's evaluated on a real-time basis by millions of people and organizations. Users connect both with people they know and those they'd like to know. Twitter users "follow" others in order to find out what they are doing, discussing, and sharing on the platform. The small bite-sized messages, sometimes referred to as micro-blogging, make it a perfect platform to share links where followers are directed to more information on your website or blog, and get people "buzzing" about your content.

Tweets typically include photos, videos, quotes, article links, and more. By tweeting, you create real-time conversations with your potential clients, peers, and other interested followers, allowing you to engage and deepen these relationships further.

Twitter has become most known as the platform for live commenting during events, or "live tweeting." This can be anything from award shows or breaking news, to televised sporting events. In the business context, live tweeting can be a marketing strategy during a conference, extending the reach of the sponsors and conference organizers' messages.

Twitter can be used in numerous ways in your business strategy. Some smartly use it for market research on specific topics or to find users who are posting about a problem that a product or service can solve. Following your peers and their Twitter feeds is also a very good defensive activity in business development. Twitter allows you to stay on top of trends in the legal field, as well as any news about competing law firms as it becomes public. All of these activities make Twitter an ideal asset within your social media tool box.

Much of the research you can do on Twitter is based on the use of what are known as hashtags. These are small text strings that create a type of overarching "sorting system" for all of the content and tweets that users are sharing on social platforms. Let's say that your target clients are entrepreneurs. If you were to add hashtags that are attractive to this target group (#entrepreneurs, #startupbusiness, #smallbusiness, etc.) and incorporate these small text strings into your tweets, entrepreneurs who are looking for information relevant to them and who perform a search using hashtags will easily find your content and tweets. If your content is relevant and valuable to that entrepreneur, they will likely choose to follow you, thus helping you to build a targeted following that's relevant to your practice.

Any information you choose to tweet is public, as Twitter is what is considered an "open" platform. This means that your tweets are visible to the world, not just your own network of followers. Someone doesn't have to have a Twitter account in order to find your tweets in Google, Bing, Yahoo, and other search engines. This adds to its usefulness, as it makes it even easier for your potential clients to find you and your content. Tweets can come up in search engine results when users search for particular keywords or topics, thus making it even more important that your content include the terms and topics you want to be associated with.

According to the survey "Social Media Update 2014" by the Pew Research Center, some 23% of online adults currently use Twitter, a statistically significant increase compared with the 18% who did so in August of 2013.[22] Twitter is particularly popular among those under 50 and the college-educated. Compared with late 2013, the service has seen significant increases among a number of varying demographic groups, including men, whites, those ages 65 and older, those who live in households with an annual household income of $50,000 or more, college graduates, and urbanites.

As for lawyers, some have found it to be an effective client attraction tool. You can use it strategically to attract targeted followers, like potential clients. One of these Twitter believers is Bob White, an attorney in Florida. He was able to attract tech companies as clients by sharing tech articles frequently via his Twitter account. He was noticed by decision makers in the tech field who could see from the content he was sharing that he knew his specialty well. Because of this, he was top of mind when they required legal counsel.

You've likely heard the saying, "we buy from and do business with the people and businesses we trust". In the graphic are some highlights about Twitter and its users about building that kind of trust.[23]

72%
of those who follow a business are more likely to make a purchase afterward from that business.

82%
of followers are more likely to recommend your product or service to friends and family.

85%
say they feel a closer connection to the business after they follow them.

85%
feel more connected to a business after following them.

86%
are likely to visit a business they follow if a friend recommends them.

Twitter allows you to connect with peers, ask or answer questions, exchange information, and create relationships quickly. In summary, Twitter can help you:

- Attract new clients
- Establish and strengthen relationships with current clients and business referrers
- Build credibility
- Drive traffic to your website and/or your blog
- Stay on top of trends and matters important to your practice
- Gain market intelligence
- Influence others to think of you as a thought leader
- Distribute news
- Promote an event or seminar
- Locate experts
- Get noticed by reporters and influential bloggers

Some lawyers question whether Twitter is an effective medium to attract new business. I say "yes" emphatically, and here's why.

Twitter users tend to be individuals who "gobble up" content and will likely engage in commenting and re-tweeting (or forwarding) your content on to their own followers.

Followers can be potential clients or can readily influence your would-be potential clients. Twitter can allow you to open a sphere of influence. As you share a tweet that contains a link to a helpful and relevant blog, whether it is your blog or someone else's, your followers and those who find it of interest will share it to their sphere of influence. That is the beauty of social networks—suddenly, your potential network and pool of potential clients opens up dramatically. This only helps in your efforts to build awareness about you and your services. In other words, it extends your marketing reach and helps solidify you as a subject matter expert. And consider this scenario: If there aren't a large number of your peers actively participating, it allows you to "own" the space around your niche and create relationships with your followers.

As you share good content of your own, such as your blog and educational information, you will be able to further attract awareness about you as an expert. Twitter is commonly used by thought leaders, major organizations, educational institutions, heads of state, and other "heavy hitters" in various fields. They often share content that has been pushed out by others on the platform that is relevant to their own target audience.

Plus, the media, bloggers, and other content curators from various fields look to Twitter for quality information to share and to identify experts as sources for news articles and blogs or to consult with on various projects or stories. By connecting with these heavy digital users via Twitter, you can become top-of-mind when they need a quote or are seeking potential speakers for their engagements or events.

These types of results can enhance your reputation as a thought leader in your field. The more your content is shared, the more you can be viewed as a trusted source of information and, in turn, grow your book of business.

Twitter also puts a human face to your legal practice, allowing others to see you as more than just a name or part of your firm. Rather, you can build the perception that you are an ally or an asset to them when the need for an attorney in your expertise arises.

Given all its potential benefits, Twitter is not a platform that should be ignored. The one challenge for new users is getting used to the language, which is comprised of shortened words, abbreviations, and acronyms. But that shouldn't stop you, because I've got a Twitter Tip Sheet that outlines those most frequently used for you, as well as a guide on how to set up your Twitter platform on my website.

> To access the Twitter Tip Sheet go to www.MicheleRuiz.com/Content-MarketingResources.

Facebook

Facebook is the quintessential social media platform actively used by well over 1.5 billion individuals and businesses, making it by far the largest and most popular of the social platforms available.[24] Through it, users connect with friends new and old and engage in a universal conversation with their social network about everything from their kids, to their sports teams, music preferences, opinions about what's going on in the world, to what they had for breakfast ... and everything in between. Besides sharing with your Facebook friends, you are also able to like and comment on items that others share. It is considered the key platform to get to know someone on a more personal level.

In this context, you are no longer just a lawyer; you may be a wife, a father, a runner, a lover of jazz, and the first to share your opinion about the latest bestseller. It is also one of the largest photo-sharing platforms online. While LinkedIn tends to be more formal and professional in tone, Facebook users typically communicate in a casual and comfortable style.

A study by the Pew Research Center reports that 71% of online adults use Facebook. Usage among seniors continues to increase, with some 56% of Internet users age 65 and older now using Facebook, up from 45% who did so in late 2013 and 35% who did so in late 2012. Women are also particularly more likely to use Facebook compared to men. Among Facebook users, the median number of Facebook friends is 155.[25]

According to the survey, Facebook users also have a wide variety of friends on the network:

- 93% of Facebook users say they are Facebook friends with family members other than parents or children
- 91% say they are Facebook friends with current friends
- 87% say they are connected to friends from the past, such as high school or college classmates
- 58% say they are connected to work colleagues
- 45% say they are Facebook friends with their parents
- 43% say they are friends with their children on Facebook
- 39% say they are connected to people they have never met in person
- 36% say they are Facebook friends with their neighbors

Facebook has been referred to as the online mass media channel because of its vast reach and availability to its users. It has utterly changed the way people communicate online. A Pew Research Center study shows that in some instances, people's main source of news and live events is via Facebook first and foremost, more so than any other online vehicle. That's even more than news media sites.[26]

Upon waking up in the morning, many users are on Facebook, scrolling through its News Feed, reading and interacting with their friends and connection's posts before they even get out of bed. Imagine the impact if news or content about you could also be part of that News Feed?

There has been a continuing upsurge of businesses and corporate entities that use Facebook to attract and open conversations with their targeted customers. For businesses, Facebook provides a way to connect to potential clients and influencers in a more personal, conversational, and less formal way. Unlike some of the other platforms, it allows for the creation of business pages, not just personal profiles, through which you can communicate the value of your business to your network and the people looking for terms related to your specialty.

Lawyers are using Facebook to promote their personal brand and connect with fans and followers in a variety of ways. These include:

- A local business page that provides an address, hours of operation, and the ability for people to "check in" when visiting your office and leave reviews
- A company page that provides information about the firm without specific details such as hours, and does not allow for reviews
- A professional profile page allowing people to follow you without connecting as "friends"
- A Facebook group dedicated to a particular interest or topics where users can request to join the group. This environment can be more private, and a place where people can collaborate and engage.

Look for my Facebook Guide at www.MicheleRuiz.com/Content MarketingResources.

Regardless of the Facebook profile option you select, the key for a successful strategy is using this powerful platform to not only provide valuable information for your target clients and influencers, but also to connect with your audience on a more personal level. It readily allows you to network with others in your profession, as well. When friends take actions, such as actively following your business page or liking your page and sharing your posts that appeal to them, it increases your visibility and potential reach to their friends who may also be potential clients. Given the propensity for legal clients to seek a referral from their network of trusted friends and colleagues, the opportunity for online "word-of-mouth" marketing is powerful with this particular platform.

By the very nature of Facebook and its communication style, you are able to drive trust and build relationships with potential clients. Sharing your enthusiasm for the New York Jets or images of you at a concert might just as easily be "liked" by a potential client as a post about the best way to set up a family trust. These likes and "shares" go a long way toward building a stronger trust level and overall affinity or connection between you and the soon-to-be-client. Also, by liking or interacting with others' content, you are demonstrating an interest in them. If you think about it, it's no different than how you build relationships offline.

One important aspect to note is that Facebook continually changes its algorithms and, therefore, you cannot assume all of your friends and followers are seeing your content organically. In fact, you should assume only a small percentage is exposed to your postings.

In order to reach a more significant portion of your target audience, you need to invest in paid advertising in the form of sponsored posts and purchased ads, and this is not an inexpensive proposition. However, given that Facebook is the largest social network in the world, reaching one in every seven people globally, and the fact that many are using this for their day-to-day communication and source of information, it's worth giving this platform some serious consideration.

Google+

I've previously mentioned that social media and technology changes at a rapid pace. Here is one example. When I started this manuscript, I wrote about Google+ and the benefits of using it. By the time I got to toward the end of the manuscript, Bradley Horowitz, a VP from Google, announced that Google is doing away with Google+ as a brand (and the assumption is Google+ as we know it is going away), and they will be introducing new products named Google Photos and Streams. And then by the time I received the manuscript back from my copy editor, it was announced on the Google Blog "Introducing the new Google+" that Google+ has been "reimagined" with Communities and Collections and it's continuing to be refined. Therefore, I'm not including information here for your business objectives at this time as it may be outdated by next week. Look for updated information on my website.

Notwithstanding that it's in redesign mode, I recommend staying on top of the changes and being open to using Google+ because simply put, it's a social platform owned by the same company that owns the largest search engine. So postings and content shared via Google+ have SEO benefits and are findable on the Internet. You can be sure Google is optimizing search results on its own social media platform over others.

Look for more information at www.MicheleRuiz.com/
ContentMarketingResources.

Instagram

We've now covered the most popular networking platforms and are ready to move on to a few more visual and artistic platforms. These photo and video sharing sites can be powerful mediums to tell stories and are wonderful tools to include in your strategy. More than 200 million users are actively sharing pictures and videos on platforms such as these, most often captured with nothing more than their smartphones.

One of the most popular photo-driven social media sites is Instagram. According to Instagram's website:

- *Instagram is a fun and quirky way to share your life with friends through a series of pictures. Snap a photo with your mobile phone, and then choose a filter to transform the image into a memory to keep around forever.*

Instagram is known for its bevy of photo editing and color filter tools, enabling you to enhance and edit your images prior to sharing them. Once images and videos have been uploaded to Instagram, the content can be shared on any number of platforms, including Facebook, Twitter, and others.

Few lawyers are using Instagram in their strategy, but depending on your target influencers or clients, it could be a goldmine of opportunity. Consider who is using Instagram on a regular basis. According to a Pew Research Center Study, 26% of online adults use Instagram, up from 17% in late 2013. Almost every demographic group saw a significant increase in the proportion of users on Instagram. Most notably, 53% of young adults ages 18-29 now use the service, compared with 37% who did so in 2013. Women are also particularly likely to be on Instagram, along with Hispanics and African-Americans, as well as those who live in urban or suburban environments.[27]

While young adults are the main audience for Instagram, this platform can open up a lawyer to a whole new world of potential clients. An example might be an attorney looking for DUI cases amongst the targeted age group with the highest rate of drunk driving incidents.[28] Highlighting legal information in optimized 15-second videos (the longest format currently allowed on Instagram) shared frequently, along with some personal photos to "get to know you better" and other related content relevant to this target age group can all be very helpful in building social relationships.

If you consider the age demographic, the fact that younger people have shorter attention spans for content and a propensity to document so much of daily life with photos and videos, it's clear why Instagram can be a fresh and different strategy. I share more on how to implement Instagram in your strategy on my downloadable Instagram Tip Sheet.

> Look for my Instagram Tip Sheet at www.MicheleRuiz.com/ ContentMarketingResources.

Pinterest

Pinterest is a visual platform, described as a place to collect and organize things you love. Some describe it as a digital scrapbook without the scissors and glue. Within the platform, you are able to organize your images or "pins" across different "boards" or areas of interest. Images and videos make up the majority of the content that is pinned, and often the images are linked to the original source, such as a blog or a website.

In terms of users, Pinterest is among the top social media platforms. It works much like other social platforms in that users can "follow" you or your boards, like your pins, and then share your pins with their social group, either on Pinterest itself, Facebook, or even Twitter. As users search the web, when they come across an image, link, story, or other interesting item, they can pin it to one of their own boards, and it gets shared with their network on the platform. Users can also upload images and links from their own computer or device.

While Pinterest started as a place to collect information on hobbies and areas of interest – especially related to fashion, travel, design, and photography – more and more businesses and brands are using it to enhance their social presence and marketing reach.

Wondering if this makes sense for attorneys to use? If you ask trial lawyer Mitch Jackson from Orange County, California, he'll strongly encourage lawyers to consider Pinterest. He's found the platform a valuable way to share his content and cross-promote from one marketing channel to another. On his board, "Legal Tips for Consumers," he's pinned links to his content, such as his eBook about wrongful death cases, podcasts targeted to victims, videos on YouTube, an infographic about personal injury, links to his blog about legal tips, and information on his community service. He also has boards related to his firm's newsletters, settlements, and verdicts, social media marketing which he champions for lawyers, books he's really enjoyed, trial lawyer tips, testimonials, and more. Besides the obvious marketing strategy, the varied types of content give followers an idea of the person he is, and not solely as it relates to what he does in his career. This type of personal branding goes a long way to building trust via this growing social media channel.

Women are the dominant users of Pinterest. According to a survey done by Comscore, over 70% of Pinterest users are female. It's a popular platform among users 18-29 and women in the age range of 30-49, as well. Recent studies show men are a growing demographic.[29]

Another key benefit of Pinterest use relates to SEO. Images shared on Pinterest can come up when someone searches in Bing, Yahoo, or Google for a term that is related to your images. If you use keywords in your board names and/or as part of your image descriptions and file names, referrers or potential clients who don't know about you could find you when one of your pins appears in the search results. Users often click on the original source of the image; and if you've set up your boards properly, and that source is your website, you've established a channel to drive people to your website and learn more about you.

For example, think how this platform might work if you specialize in asbestos claims. You could use Pinterest to post images and links to content about all things asbestos, including mesothelioma cancer caused by asbestos poisoning, various treatments, different types of asbestos, where it can be found in your home, support and encouragement content, as well as content you create that is relevant to your target clients about your legal services. This can include your videos, blogs, and other content, all optimized for search purposes, meaning you've used keywords. By optimizing Pinterest in these ways, you can see how this could help your lead generation.

Jackson has found that new clients often say they first learned about him in a video or a photo posted on Pinterest. If it's helping him bring in new clients, it might work for your practice.

Check out my Pinterest Tip Sheet on my website.

Look for my Pinterest Tip Sheet at www.MicheleRuiz.com/Content-MarketingResources.

YouTube

While people usually think of YouTube as a source for content, I've included it here as a social platform because YouTube also allows you to create channels with followers, known in this instance as subscribers. Early on, this video-sharing platform became synonymous with homemade funny cat videos, also referred to as user-generated content, as opposed to slick, professionally produced content. But it has since evolved into a tremendously valuable marketing tool as consumers' appetites for video content is growing exponentially on every screen – TVs, computers, smartphones, and tablets.

You may be familiar with certain marketing videos that have gone "viral" on YouTube. One is the low-cost cult video series "Will It Blend," created by the blender manufacturer Blendtec. Another is the "Dollar Shave Club" video, now topping over 17 million views. I mention them here because some people think of these types of videos when YouTube marketing is mentioned. But the majority of businesses – large and small – succeeding with the integration of video into their marketing strategy never hit anywhere near those types of numbers, nor are they creating humorous videos. They're succeeding because the content is informational, relevant, and of value to their target audience. And more often than not, the videos aren't professionally produced by an expensive production or marketing company.

Attorneys and legal firms are starting to recognize the benefits of the exposure and opportunities YouTube provides. Some of these law firms are creating video content in-house with dedicated staff and equipment. Others, in particular smaller firms and individual lawyers, are using webcams or even their smartphones to create compelling content, or using outside production companies to help.

In either instance, implementing a YouTube channel is much like creating your own TV network, with the potential to grow a following. People who really like videos on a particular subject will often subscribe to You-Tube channels to get an email alert every time a new video is uploaded on one of their favorite channels. This has proved to be very effective in creating brand awareness and driving traffic to websites.

Latham & Watkins has a YouTube Channel demonstrating a varied strategy. If you visit their YouTube channel, you'll see:

- Videos called "Get to Know Us" to introduce the firm
- Informational videos about Asia restructurings, economic policy and regulatory reform, and the energy sector
- Feel-good interviews with employees
- Videos about their pro bono work and community service
- Newsmaker videos highlighting their attorneys who have been in the news
- Light-hearted "Word of the Day" M&A Jargon videos

Other examples include Jones Day, which shares video-recorded webinars on topics such as environmental rule changes for businesses, tax reform updates, and ten things you need to know about California employment law. Another example of a firm using the platform well is Fenwick & West, which shares presentations from Fenwick attorneys and even a playful holiday video.

With one billion people visiting YouTube worldwide every month, video marketing can be a growth strategy for law firms.[30] Potential clients are often landing on a YouTube video after using a search engine to find information. A video with the right keywords bubbles up as an option on the results page, and they are suddenly watching your content. Consider that YouTube is another platform owned by Google, and, therefore, it's not surprising that videos show up prominently in search engine results. Some people will opt to follow your channel and get notified when you upload more videos.

Think of all of the potential topics for your short videos—the possibilities are endless. Similar to Facebook and LinkedIn, people can engage either by liking a video or commenting. Some will ask questions and you can respond, further demonstrating your expertise and allowing you to engage with the potential client. Further, this string of comments can persuade others to take note of your videos.

YouTube is an underutilized platform that I highly recommend for lawyers to use for client attraction. I cover more on how to create good quality videos with easy-to-use equipment and this marketing strategy in the chapter called Pulling a Content Marketing Strategy Together. You can also download my YouTube Tip Sheet to set up your YouTube Channel and watch my video on how to shoot videos clients will want to watch on my website. If you're camera shy and don't think you'll come across well in a video, I've got you covered. I share tips I've given hundreds of people I've interviewed on-camera during my days as a TV anchor. I also share a checklist to help you prepare to create videos.

> Look for tips about YouTube and creating videos at
> www.MicheleRuiz.com/ContentMarketingResources.

SlideShare

SlideShare is a platform initially created for sharing presentations with a large community of viewers. Since its inception and growth in popularity, PDFs, infographics, videos and other content can now be uploaded, as well. The site boasts over 60 million visitors a month and houses over 15 million uploads on every type of topic imaginable, including of course legal matters.

Much like other social platforms, SlideShare allows users to comment, like, and interact with your content. You also have a profile page in which you can list your practice, your specialties, and information about you and your firm in more detail. Content uploaded into the SlideShare platform (also known as SlideShares) can also be embedded into other's websites or blogs and can be shared on Facebook, LinkedIn, Twitter, and other social platforms you're using, making it a perfect repository for your content.

A great example of this platform in action can be seen with the global law firm DLA Piper, which uses SlideShare as a marketing tool. If you follow the firm, you'll find they use well-produced infographics to share knowledge on a variety of topics, including the Affordable Care Act and its implications for employers. The firm strategically uses the transcript section, as well, to provide more detailed information about the topic.

Given the large audience to be found at SlideShare, it is another useful channel through which your potential clients might find you. Another advantage is that, for the most part, SlideShare is geared toward businesses, much like LinkedIn. If you use the PRO version of SlideShare, you can implement a built-in lead capture form whenever someone wants to download your presentation. This can help your marketing strategy by allowing you to later reach out to those who have shown interest in your content. The platform also includes a full analytics suite that helps you understand more about your viewers and the traffic to your shared content, including a snapshot of the last 1,000 views and more information about those users.

When you think of disseminating your content in a variety of formats in various places on the Internet, SlideShare is an underused platform that can provide a good impression about your expertise.

For more information on how to create compelling SlideShares, take a look at the section about presentations in the Content chapter.

I've put together some key marketing strategies for SlideShare which is available on my website.

> Look for more information on SlideShare at www.MicheleRuiz.com/ContentMarketingResources.

7 Impactful Content Creation and Distribution Strategies

In a digital world, in order to convert prospects into clients and clients into referrers, you need to produce great content that is "findable" online. Followers will become evangelists, and new clients will come to you.

With the array of web-based tools available and the help of some pretty inexpensive equipment at your disposal, it has never been easier to create compelling content. As I covered earlier, content is anything created and subsequently uploaded to a site online. Content marketing is sharing valuable content you've published, as well as other people's content.

In this chapter, you'll learn what is most important to keep in mind for strategic business purposes. I also describe various forms of content and how they can be used to attract future clients. Most important, you'll learn how to create the various kinds of content I've discussed along with tips and know-how from my experience as a journalist on leveraging your work to make the most of your efforts. All of this will help you decide what to prioritize in order to meet your objectives.

You're Not in the Legal Business

First things first: when discussing a successful content strategy, you need to get a glass of wine, take a sip, then say out loud, "I am not in the legal business. I am in the business of being of value." Say it like you mean it. Again. Until you believe it.

Everything you do online should always be client centric. When you think of what you've learned about traditional marketing, you are probably inclined to start with a "sell." Sell your services. Sell your firm. Sell the size of your firm. Sell where you obtained your law degree. Sell your case wins. Sell your years of experience.

This "sales-ey" approach won't work well today. Social media users don't want to be advertised to. Trust me. There are reams of data that support this. They really don't care about your services. What they care about is how you are able to:

- Solve their problem
- Help them avoid a problem
- Make them smarter
- Improve their life
- Improve their business
- Save them money
- Save them time
- Save them stress
- Save their marriage

It's all about them - not about you. They don't care to hear why you're the best, the brightest, the most experienced, or their best option. That can be conveyed implicitly. Here's the secret: if you prioritize the substance of your content on your potential clients' needs, they will come to the conclusion that you are the right choice for them, or for someone they know in need of your services. In the end, this is what is most valuable for your client acquisition and retention goals.

Content, regardless of what kind, should share or solve, not sell. You want to be viewed as a reliable and valuable source of information, with content that is created in the format that target clients prefer to ingest and found on the platforms that resonate best with them. This might be blogs shared via Twitter, videos hosted on YouTube and shared on your website, or any other number of ways your audience uses to receive and view your content. The content should be crafted using your clients' own words, not "legalese." In a client-centric content marketing strategy, you are a giver, not a promoter or a seller.

CLIENT CENTRIC APPROACH

While an altruistic approach, being a resource has the added benefit of leading many to follow you for the value of the content you are sharing. If you remember the client acquisition funnel in chapter 4, once potential clients are following and engaged with you, you're building a relationship with them. It's the "likeability" factor. Your "giving" pays you back with clients who will contact you when they have a need or with those who will refer someone who needs your expertise. Also, don't forget to consider the lifetime value of those relationships.

The biggest hurdle in implementing a content marketing strategy for attorneys, as it is for many embarking on this work, is figuring out where to start. I assure you, if you're adept at talking to people, you can create impactful content. In this chapter, along with additional resources I have for you online I will show you how.

Your Voice

One of the most important elements of your content marketing and online content will be the "voice" or tone in which it is created. In other words, how will you speak to your target audience? Early in my broadcasting career, I was taught by a voice coach to imagine seeing your best friend through the camera lens when you are reading the teleprompter, and imagining having a conversation with him or her. This tactic helps a news anchor come across conversationally and builds up your likeability factor with your audience. Sure enough, it really worked and went a long way in developing a feeling amongst my viewers that they could trust me. I even had people who I had never met tell me that they felt as if I was a friend in their living room with them.

This tactic can work just as well with the content you create. Your "voice," or how you say what you say, should read or sound as if you're having a conversation with your best friend and are simply sharing some information he or she doesn't know. Avoid being verbose and speaking "legalese" so you don't alienate your potential clients by coming across as pompous or arrogant. The only exception to this is if your target clients are comfortable with this style, such as other lawyers who are in-house counsel. Your tone and the words you choose should be friendly, approachable, and conversational. Using your clients' vernacular demonstrates that you understand their issues and is an immediate way to connect with them. In the media world, we refer to this as speaking "human."

Remember, when writing your online content that this is NOT the time to create a dissertation nor a legal opinion or brief, unless that is exactly the type of content you are writing. The reader, or viewer if it's video content you're working with, should feel like you're sitting down over lunch with them and discussing their needs and pain points. There's a fine line between speaking "lawyer-ese" versus coming across as knowledgeable and yet relatable. Your purpose here is to develop relationships, and in order to do so, you should sound like a trusted friend, rather than a sales-ey attorney.

Content Types

Assuming you've followed the chapters of this book in order, you now know who your target audiences are and where to find them online, as well as the tone to use and how best to communicate with them. The next step in the process is to become clear on what content types you should use to convey your messages and build relationships with your potential clients. Any information you create and publish, regardless of its format, is considered content, and in this section, I go over some of the most commonly used types of digital content.

As you can see from the graphic, your content will and should be created in a variety of formats, even if it's just two or three kinds. The idea is to be found where your target clients are and they're in various places online so you want to sprinkle content all over the Internet. You also want to provide them content in their preferred formats. As mentioned earlier, you want to be consistent with your messaging, even though you are creating that message in different formats.

In the following section, you'll find the basics about content types: what they are, the business benefits of each, and how to create them. We have included information on how to integrate each type into your strategy and discern their effectiveness later in the strategy chapter.

Blogs

A blog is a website that is maintained by an individual or a small group, with journal-type entries and commentary. It can include expert insights, descriptions of events, photos and videos, and opinion or satire pieces. Blogs are typically displayed in order by date, with latest "posts" or entries listed first, and move chronologically. Blogs have evolved over time, and now not only include individuals as their authors, but also large entities with multiple contributors, such as corporations, large law firms, non-profits, and even aggregator type sites, such as the *Huffington Post.*

For lawyers, blog posts can greatly benefit your content strategy and should be the cornerstone of your content arsenal. The idea is to begin with a strong blog post and then push it out by linking to it on various social platforms. This enables you to share your thoughts, ideas, and analysis, while drawing potential clients to you. Also, you can use the blog's content to promote other content you've created, such as webinars, SlideShares, or videos on the same topic. Blogs are also one of the best ways to become known as a thought leader, as we'll discuss later in this book.

Most often, blogs are created as either a part of your regular website or as a stand-alone blog on a blogging platform. Web solutions are an option if your website does not already have the availability to add a blog to it. Some to consider are: Wordpress, Blogspot, Blogger, Squarespace, and TypePad.

Once you've reviewed a few of the platforms above and have chosen the best one for your needs, getting started is as easy as creating an account, setting up the name of your blog, and sitting down and writing your first entry or post.

To get started, go through this checklist:

- What's the purpose of your blog? Is it to inform, motivate, educate?
- What goals are you trying to achieve?
- What problem does it solve or help avoid for your target audience?
- What is your focus? For example, all aspects of sports law or specifically the collegiate level?
- What is your publishing schedule? Once a week, once a day, etc.?
- Will you consistently use pictures or video within your blog? If so, where will you be getting those?
- How will you be handling comment moderation? There are plug-ins for blog platforms that will allow you to monitor, pre-screen, and comment in an easy way.

You can and should add images, videos, if available, checklists, links to interesting content that you'd like to share, and of course, your web signature, including all of your relevant social connection and contact information.

Here's a secret to easily create blogs time efficiently, as well as ensuring your voice is conversational. Once you've selected a topic and a headline, write down three ideas about that topic. Then use a recording device such as the dictation software on your smartphone and the notes feature. Simply start talking about those three points so that what you're saying is written out while you're speaking. Remember to imagine while you do this that you're talking to a friend. When you're done, you'll have the first draft of your blog. Now go back and edit the "umm's," "ah's," and other disfluencies. Include a standard ending and signature to each blog, and you're off and running.

The reality is, you already have the knowledge in your head that you want to share. This is just a quick and easy method to get it out of your head and into a written format. Here's an example of how that would work: Let's say you've settled on the topic *Top Three Ways to Avoid Trouble with the IRS*.

First, write down a note for each one of the top three ways, in order to help you stay on track. Then go to your notes application on your smartphone, tap the microphone, and imagine you're talking to your best friend. You'll start by saying something like,

"When clients come to me with a tax problem, often it's related to three common issues. (*refer to your note*) One, it's the.......... In that case, that could have been avoided if the individual had....... (*refer to your note*). Another typical mistake I see is .... This can usually be resolved by .... (*refer to your note*) And another common issue or problem stems from .... In this scenario, a person can .... You should consult with a tax lawyer if you're having a problem and aren't sure what to do."

End your blog post with a question that can be posted as well, can be effective in order to encourage people to interact with your blog.

Send that note to yourself and proceed to edit and clean it up. Add it to your blog template, which should include a standard signature that might look something like:

Bob Greene, Greene and Associates Tax Attorney

From here, add a call to action, a disclaimer about advertising, and links to social profiles to your signature. Note that some blogging platforms have a plug-in or an app to standardize a signature line.

Once you've done this process a few times, you can get to a point where you're completing a blog post in 15 minutes or so. Allocate an hour a week, and you've got 4 blog posts to publish and push out based on the schedule you've determined. Be sure to have a consistent place where you jot down ideas for blog posts as they come to you so you can easily go back to them when you're ready to write.

Want more tips? Go to my website to download my blog template to help you craft ideas and take everything into consideration to get the largest number of views possible.

Download a blog template at www.MicheleRuiz.com/ ContentMarketingResources.

Videos

As a tangent to blogs, you can also create your blog in the form of a video. Vlogs, as these are sometimes called, are similar to blogs, but you actually record the information as a piece of video content rather than written content. By creating a library of videos you are also able to easily distribute and promote them through platforms we discussed earlier, such as YouTube.

The usage of video can be a powerful pillar of your content strategy. As people search the web to learn, video is a top content type to find answers regardless of what type of business you are working to promote. Videos for the professional service providers can be used to:

- Inform
- Educate
- Instruct
- Entertain
- Influence
- Brand
- Promote
- Recruit

Many lawyers today are maximizing the usage of video blogging. Social Security attorney Andrew Kinney, of Minnesota firm, Hoglund, Chwialkow-ski & Mrozik, has a video named "Top 5 Ways to Get Approved for Social Security Benefits," which has garnered almost 57,000 views. Cincinnati Social Security lawyer Anthony Castelli has a video on his YouTube Channel called "3 Critical Mistakes That Can Ruin Your Social Disability Claim" that has over 97,000 views. Both videos are shot very simply with webcams or consumer video cameras with no fancy editing or graphics included. By creating simple, informative, high-value content on topics their target clients want to know about, these lawyers have been able to garner a huge number of video views and recognition for their firms in a few easy steps.

Since both lawyers have included the links to their main websites within the description of the videos, those videos, created just one time, are continuously influencing potential clients to click on the links and find out more about their firms. The marketing success they are experiencing is not about the quality of these video productions, but rather about the quality of the information.

Wondering what other kinds of videos you might create? Why not explore:

- Recorded webinars
- Employee videos that convey what it's like to work at the firm

- Expert presentations
- Recorded speeches
- Client testimonials
- Firm introductions
- Short educational or informational videos about complex topics
- Frequently asked questions (and their answers)
- Updates on changes in the law
- A summary of your services or expertise
- Decision-making videos that can help a client through the decision-making process, such as *How to Choose a Civil Rights Lawyer*
- Case results
- Attorney recognitions

With a little creativity, there is no limit to the types of videos you can create. These videos can go a long way toward garnering trust and building relationships with your target audience. The making of video content is not as difficult as some people fear. The advent of easy-to-use cameras and devices, including those on smartphones and tablets, makes creating video content quite simple, and thinking it's challenging shouldn't stop you from trying this powerful content type.

While you can hire a production company to shoot your video content, for the purposes of video blogs as discussed here, if you're inclined to, you can do this yourself. That is if you're not focused on implementing highly produced videos for branding and marketing purposes which larger firms tend to invest in. As mentioned earlier with video blogs, the quality of the information and how it's delivered is the key, versus the snazziness of a sophisticated video production. With some ingenuity and a simple device that you probably already have in hand, you are well on your way to increasing the viral potential of your content as well as the success of your social program.

What you'll need to have:

- **A camera.** Try the webcam on your computer or laptop, or using your smartphone, especially the newer iterations, on a stand so it's steady. You can also buy a consumer video camera for a few hundred dollars. If you do so, make sure to get a tripod for it, again in order to keep it steady.
- **Decent lighting.** Your face should not be in the dark in your video content. Your audience wants to see your face clearly. Make sure you

have lights on around you or good natural light on your face. You can also buy a small lighting kit and add it to the top of your video camera.

- **Good audio.** If you're using the microphone from your webcam, smartphone or video camera, make sure you are recording in a quiet area so your voice can be heard clearly. When there is a lot of ambient noise competing with what you're saying, it can turn your audience off. You can also purchase a lavaliere or small clip-on microphone to use with a video recorder that you can easily clip on yourself if background noise is an issue. External microphones for smartphones are being introduced into the marketplace, as well.
- **Uncluttered background.** Be mindful of what is showing up behind and around you. Make sure it's not too cluttered and that there isn't a book in the background with a distracting title or a plant leaf that appears to be sticking out of your head.
- **Editing software.** While this is not absolutely necessary, it can be very helpful to add some simple graphics to your videos, such as your name and contact information. Most computers, laptops, and mobile devices come equipped with basic editing software which is all you really need for these purposes. You can also purchase them for nominal amounts.

If you have all of the above you're set to start creating your video content today.

Now let's figure out how to get your expert knowledge recorded. Your preparation should include answering the following questions:

- Why are you creating the video and what specific problem are you addressing?
- Who are you talking to?
- What do you want your audience to know and do when they're done viewing the video?
- What is the call to action?

Refer back to the blog section earlier in this chapter on how to create topics for blogs with three ideas. The construct of your videos should be similar, including having a beginning, middle and end. The beginning of the video should address what you're talking about. The middle is comprised of your three points, and the end is the summary sentence and a call to action. Don't be afraid to add a story to illustrate your point or some humor, if that comes naturally to you.

The key to creating successful video blogs is not about perfection. Don't get stuck on re-recording it 15 times because you feel your delivery is not perfect. As mentioned in the tone section, you want to come across in a conversational manner. Imagine talking to new client who just came into your office. Your audience isn't looking for perfection. They are looking for valuable information, as well as an expert they can trust and relate to. An occasional 'um' or other normal things you say when you're having a conversation is, in fact, perfectly imperfect.

Remember to keep your videos short, simple and focused - two to three minutes in length is ideal. Don't try to cram everything you know about a topic in one video. Instead, think about creating multiple short videos around a topic. User behavior has changed and more and more people video "snack," and don't have the patience to watch a 15-minute video unless they're binge watching their favorite TV series on Netflix.

Here's the secret to leveraging your investment of time spent creating video blogs to develop more content. Once you've recorded a video blog, have the video transcribed and use the transcription as the basis for a blog post. Or take the audio track from the video and using your editing software, create a podcast of the soundtrack. Be creative and use the information in as many fashions as possible in order to gain the most from your efforts.

Video content is by far one of the most engaging types of content you can distribute. Creating, posting, and sharing educational or informative videos for your clients, peers, and potential target audience is one of the best ways to show yourself as a thought leader in your niche. When people can see and hear you speak on a subject, it goes a long way in positioning you as a trusted resource for your audience. If done well, you'll influence people's impression of you through the usefulness of the videos you distribute. For a checklist to help you prepare to record your videos visit my website. I also have a video called Seven Newscast Tips to Be an Engaging Presenter for you on how to be an engaging presenter based on my experience as a TV news anchor.

Download a video production checklist and access the video Seven Newscast Tips to Be an Engaging Presenter at www.MicheleRuiz.com/ContentMarketingResources.

Podcasts

As mentioned briefly in the last section, you can distribute audio-only files known as podcasts as well as videos. These audio files are made available on the Internet for users to either download to their player, computer, or favorite device. Often, podcasts are made into a series and users can subscribe and get new "installments" as they become available. Podcasting, as it is called, is basically a form of audio broadcast or radio on demand, over the Internet in a downloadable fashion. Video podcasts are also becoming popular which is a video clip offered in a similar fashion as a subscription to an ongoing program.

According to Apple, iTunes® podcast subscriptions reached over 1 billion in 2013, and continue to grow.[31] Podcasts can be easily accessed by busy people as they are driving or working out. They are often overlooked as marketing content, yet have proven to be successful for many, including Kevin O'Neill, a partner at Patton Boggs law firm in Washington, D.C. Proof in point, his popular public policy podcast has led to several speaking engagements and even his own radio show on the Voice America Business network.

Podcasts provide lawyers an opportunity to reach a wider audience because of their ease of accessibility via the users' preferred device. If your podcast gets a strong following, it can be a very effective way to build your client base while being both cost and time efficient.

Some content developers use simple mobile apps and they record via their smartphones to create smartphone podcasts. There are also avid podcasters who use the following types of equipment or tools:

- A microphone and a stand to get good audio quality
- Headphones for interviewing someone, in order to eliminate feedback
- Audio recording and editing software in order to capture the recording and to edit out any mistakes or bloopers, as well as to edit in an opening and closing "slate" or statement
- An audio mixer to use if you're interviewing several people. When more than one person is involved in the podcast, people typically use Skype
- Some type of publishing capability, such as iTunes®, or third-party listening apps

Some podcasting pros even live-stream while recording their podcasts. While there is no limit on how long a podcast can be, according to statistics, people's attention span lasts between 10-18 minutes when listening to audio. There are many software options, some free and some subscription-based, that can be used to record and edit your audio files. The options available continue to grow and evolve, thus it's best to do some research online before getting started to be sure you have the most appropriate tool for your needs.

Just remember, podcasts require some practice in order to pull all the elements together and create them well and in the short amounts of time needed to make them optimal. However, they are becoming more mainstream, and if talking into a microphone is more appealing than writing or recording yourself on video, consider these to be a great way to build trust before a potential client has ever met you.

Webinars, Online Seminars, and Live Virtual Events

A virtual event or webinar is very much like any one of the in-person seminars that you have likely attended. However, rather than being face-to-face with the presenter and the other attendees, everyone joins through a computer or device and dials in to a common conference line or an online conferencing platform. The most common ones are subscription options such as WebEx™, GoToWebinar™, and Adobe Connect™. A free option for the presenter is Google Hangouts On Air™. Participants listen to the presenter via a conference line or online microphone. Some online events are even set up so participants can see the presenters via cameras.

If an online presentation is being used, the attendees will see a PowerPoint or other slide deck on their screens while listening to the seminar's host. Additionally, whichever webinar tool you've chosen to use will likely include a question and answer interface available to the attendees to use during the presentation. Q&As keep presentations interesting and the attendees engaged, so don't be afraid to use this element. Webinars, much like video content, can also be recorded, and the recordings and audio files then used later as additional content to be shared.

The biggest benefit of hosting online events or webinars is their effectiveness in garnering qualified prospects. This marketing tactic can be extremely effective as the attendees are typically very engaged, sometimes more so than with a blog or social media content. If a webinar is done well, it will engage the attendees with a more intimate communication style. They are able to hear and/or see the experts present and even interact with them. From a communications perspective, this type of deeper interaction builds your credibility faster than by simply reading a blog or clicking on a link you've posted and shared.

Depending on the topic, you can use the webinar setting to identify pain points and issues for your potential clients and address them right then and there. Or you might choose to use that information as a springboard for more content. You will be able to highlight your expertise and convey your understanding of the problems and solutions you suggest.

Another great aspect of webinars and online events is the data you can access about how engaged your attendees are and how many drop off during the presentation. Also, most solutions allow you to capture information about your attendees that can be more difficult to gather with other types of content sharing, such as their email, title, and contact phone number, allowing you to more easily reach out to them and convert them from leads to clients. Some webinar hosts that have larger audiences even go so far as to charge a small fee to their webinar attendees, turning the online events into an additional source of revenue.

Webinars are also incredibly efficient. They not only deliver in-depth content that helps build the credibility of your practice and brand, but do so with very little cost involved. There is no room or venue to rent, no electronics to supply, nor any large number of attendees to facilitate. You also don't have to limit the number of people who can attend. With today's technologies, hosting a webinar can be as easy as picking up your smartphone and dialing in.

When building your arsenal of content, any effort that can be leveraged and molded into multiple uses is worth investigating. Webinars have the benefit of the content being used directly during the webinar, and then any elements, such as SlideShares or PowerPoints that are used can be shared as highly valuable content. See my recommendation to create handouts from PowerPoint content in the next section.

The transcripts from the webinar are also good audio files and can easily be used for podcasting. The ideas held within it can be the basis for a few blog posts, a great article or guest blog, or an eBook. You can even easily video record the webinar and then provide the link to that video to share with those who weren't able to attend live. There are even software options where you can re-run webinars at scheduled times in the future. With so many options to leverage your work, you can see how one idea can come to great use in a myriad of ways.

For existing clients, webinars and online events can be a great way to keep them engaged and updated on the types of specialties your firm provides. It's a good "top of mind" strategy.

Once you've decided to create a webinar, there are some important steps to hosting a successful event that you'll want to remember.

First, choose the topic you'll be covering. Your target audience has a large number of issues they are contending with. Given what you know about their needs, pick one that you believe they'd want to learn more about and then think about how you can help with these issues. What do you want the key take-away to be at the end of your presentation? Your goal should be to educate and be considered a resource who builds trust with your target audience.

Webinars or online seminars typically follow one of two formats. The first is tactical, as in presenting step-by-step how-to information. Another is informational or some version of analysis of trends or changes in laws or regulations. For example, the Norton Rose Fulbright law firm conducts a monthly web seminar series on topics such as "Trends in Energy Disputes" or "Risk, Benefits and Steps to Take When a Company is in the Cloud."

Choosing a title is a very important step. Be as descriptive as possible, going for a title that clearly conveys what will be presented, versus a vague, yet clever, one. Ambiguous or confusing titles can lead to low turnout or dissatisfied attendees. Make sure the title of the webinar and the marketing copy you write to describe it is as inviting and interesting as possible. Also, highlight who the perfect person to attend might be, so you don't have the wrong audience signing up, which can lead to disappointment or dissatisfaction and a bad reputation in short order.

Next, you'll want to set up a way for your attendees to register and later log in to the webinar or event. There are registration tools, such as GoToWebinar, that help with all aspects of this, from hosting the webinar itself, to setting up the landing page where your attendees will find out more information. Give specific information on these pages about the benefits to your audience. These benefits are conveyed with phrases that start like

- You will learn…
- Know how to…

- You will see...
- Find out how...
- Discover...

From here, create your invitation email for all of the potential attendees and post information about the webinar details on your various social media platforms. On the registration page, consider encouraging people to ask their most pressing questions on the topic, which will help you as you consider the content of your presentation.

Now that you've invited attendees, it's time to prepare for the presentation itself. Boring webinars are often snoozers, not because of the content, but because of how it is delivered to the audience. Speakers and hosts matter – a lot – to the success of a presentation. Do you plan to give the presentation by yourself, or would it help to have other speakers participate with you and potentially even a moderator? Either format is fine; what is important here is the presentation style.

How people sound during the webinar is critical to achieving your goals. The experts should speak clearly, be engaging and conversational, and come across confidently. If you have guests, feel free to have light banter and keep the tone conversational, as that makes the audience less likely to tune out the webinar. A moderator can be an active participant and introduced to the audience, or mostly silent, assisting you as needed by fielding questions that are being asked and bringing them to your attention at the right time during the online seminar.

Presentation style is critical. Remember, boring or dull means you've wasted your time and you're not getting the most from the resources you've spent time creating and marketing the webinar. Check out my Seven Newscast Tips to Be an Engaging Presenter video on my website for surefire ways to make your audience tune-in.

Also, be sure to evaluate your technology needs. Make sure your camera and audio equipment is of decent quality, as the audience is relying on the audio, and you'll want to be sure they are able to clearly hear the presentation. You'll also want to make sure you have an excellent Internet connection and speed when you'll be hosting your webinar.

Before you hold your first online seminar, have a plan in place for what you will do with the materials after it is over. Consider recording it and letting people access it on-demand from your website. If this is in your plan, be sure you make the necessary arrangements to capture the recording.

Many of the webinar tools we've mentioned offer recording options, so that might be your best bet for ease of use. I offer more tips on how to use recorded webinars and the content from them in the downloadable Virtual Presentation Tip Sheet available on my website.

The next step is creating the presentation materials. As for the actual slides to use during your webinar, I offer more specific guidance on how to create compelling PowerPoints and SlideShares in the next section.

> Download a Virtual Presentation Tip Sheet at www.MicheleRuiz.com/ ContentMarketingResources.

Slides, PowerPoints and Presentations

You, like me, have probably sat through too many presentations with hard-to-read dense text and excruciatingly boring slides. Some presenters put words on a PowerPoint and just read them, which I call "Death by PowerPoint." And as presentations are a very common tool used in the legal field, these types of boring presentations are more the norm. As mentioned in the webinar section, visual communication is critical to a successful presentation. Anyone can create a PowerPoint with facts and figures and read from the slides. In fact, if that's what you're inclined to do, save everyone's time and just cancel the presentation and send the slides. Please, do not present in front of a group by simply reading your slides.

Slide presentations that are done well are excellent content that can be leveraged in a multitude of ways for bringing in clients. Savvy presenters are taking information, concepts, and solutions, together with tools on the market, and incorporating interactive and multimedia enhancements into their slides. There are engaging elements available to you, such as video, music, images, colors, and animations. Even still, sometimes the most effective presentations are clean, with high-quality imagery, few words and good storytelling.

As both a professional speaker and a professional storyteller, I know the impact a well prepared slide deck that supports your presentation can have on your target audience. It does wonders to reinforce the perception of you as a thought leader. Tom Peter, in his "Presentation Excellence" article, says, "An effective speech to 1,000 people is 1,000 intimate 1-on-1 conversations."[32]

Slide presentations can be very powerful, mainly for the following reasons:

- Visuals can make both the topic and the presenter more memorable
- Presentation materials made available online are a great way to educate people who could not attend or join the webinar about your expertise. Engaging presentations can teach, inspire, and influence an audience

You may already have presentations prepared. With some adjustments, they can be adapted for an effective content marketing strategy and help build your content library.

The most common program used today to create presentations is Microsoft's PowerPoint, but there are others, as well. Apple users often use Keynote, and those who prefer cloud-based applications look to Prezi. As would be expected, creating slides varies slightly with each software type. (If you need help figuring out how to use any of these, I recommend the educational website Lynda.com as a resource.)

No matter which one you use, the following considerations are essential when thinking of your slide presentations:

- Who is your audience?
- What is their background?
- What's their problem or challenge?
- What is their level of knowledge?
- What do you want them to do?
- What is your point?
- Why does it matter to them?
- What is the key takeaway you want your audience to remember?

By answering these questions you're putting yourself in the shoes of your attendees. This is important when you want to be persuasive. I've attended a presentation by a scientist who was speaking to an audience comprised of people who were not specialists in his field. His presentation was highly technical, and he used words that were esoteric and foreign to most of us. Inevitably, those in the audience who were not experts didn't understand much of what was being presented. Unfortunately, he failed to connect with the audience. Think of all the time he spent preparing, traveling, and presenting, and then add to that audience members' time. Everyone felt like their time was wasted in attending, and I'm sure he probably sensed that discontent when very few questions were asked. This kind of disastrous disconnect can alienate your target clients. So keeping your audience in mind is critical to achieving your goals.

The next step is thinking of a story that illustrates your point and why it matters. Stories are so important to make your presentations compelling, relatable, and memorable - hey can be very persuasive, as well. A good story that triggers an emotion makes the message stick.

Facts and information are not enough to draw clients to you primarily. With the Internet readily available, anyone can find the information they want. So how do you stand out? You want to connect with your audience on a human level. Telling a story is one of the ways to do that, as it allows your personality to emerge.

When adding stories into your mix, be sure to put key ideas in terms that your clients can visualize in order to connect with them. You've heard "Show, Don't Tell" when preparing presentations. Provide examples, case studies, analogies, benefits, and conclusions to demonstrate the story.

Struggling with how to develop a story? Here are key components:

- The problem or challenge
- Cause of the problem or challenge (give examples your audience can relate to)
- How and why you solved (show and tell the audience your experience) or demonstrate impact (in a way your attendees can relate to)

Once you've thought about adding a story, then focus on the structure of your presentation. A common one for informational presentations is:

- Introduction
- What you'll learn
- Content
- Call to action
- Q&A

Then think of your presentation in three parts:

1. Slides your clients and potential clients will see
2. Notes only you will see
3. Handout your audience will receive

Slides: When preparing your slides, keep them simple.

- Slides should reinforce your words, not repeat them.
- They should add structure to your story. Keep the graphics to a minimum.
- Avoid charts with hard-to-read data and details. Eliminate details that are not essential to your presentation. When in doubt, leave it out. Remember, you can include details in handouts you can provide your audience.
- Avoid bullet points, if and when you can. Consider other ways to demonstrate your point. If you do use bullet points, keep them to a minimum and avoid more than one or two slides with bullet points.
- Write the copy as headlines, not complete sentences and limit each to five or six words. Bullet points can lead to bad habits, like reading your slides, and more often than not, they are boring to your audience.
- Substitute images for text. Use high quality photos. Bad quality photos communicate a negative message to your audience.

Go to my website for a list of online resources for high-resolution photos readily available to use.

INCORPORATE CLEAN EASY-TO-READ GRAPHICS

Notes: When adding notes, remember that notes are meant to be visible only to you in order to guide you through the presentation. In PowerPoint, this is done in the Notes format. Professional speakers often memorize their story and don't use notes. However, I don't discourage using and referring to notes, as long as you avoid reading from them.

A news trick to help you sound conversational is to use bullet points rather than using full sentences for your notes so you can speak to the ideas. In that way, you're not tempted to read and will come across more conversational.

 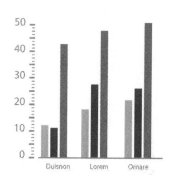

Handouts: This is a "leave-behind" or even better, a "send-later" document. Preparing a detailed document to share after your presentation frees you up so you won't feel compelled to say and share minute details in your talk. That way, you are able to focus on what is most important for that audience and at the same time keep your slides simple. This makes it easier for attendees to review and remember both what was presented and who you are as the presenter.

Note that I'm not recommending you print out your slides and provide them before your presentation as some do. Slides are to support you as an expert and a presenter, and giving out slides as a handout can be a distraction. Further, if you follow these recommendations, your slides won't be a stand-alone piece. I'm referring to a prepared handout with key information that you want to share.

If you follow this three-part formula, it can help you avoid the mistake of putting too much information on your slides. You want your audience to be hungry for more of your expertise.

After you complete the first draft of your story, go back and edit by asking yourself the following:

- Is everything I've included in the presentation important for the audience to know or to show how smart I am? If the latter is the case, take parts of it out.

- Are my examples, analogies, and case studies strong enough to support the main ideas? If not, replace them with others.
- Have I put myself in the audience members' shoes? Do I use the words "we" and "us"? Nix out as many "I's" and "You's" as possible.
- Are the data and study results I use easy to comprehend and visualize? For example, journalist Lev Grossman used this visual to talk about a Facebook stat: "If Facebook were a country, it would be the third largest, behind only China and India."[33]

Now let's cover the ending. Your final slides should support your takeaway message or call to action. Sometimes that can be accomplished with one slide; other times it might take two or three. When you're thinking of attracting clients, summarize and then remind them of what they need to do or think, or the benefits of working with you. If appropriate, remind them of the actions you want them to take. Last, the final slide should include your contact information and photograph.

When you're done, review the entire presentation. Keep in mind that the goal is not to create a great presentation. The goal is to connect with your audience. If you do go deeply into your online presentations, be sure to add analytics so that you can understand what parts of the content users engage with the most online. Then optimize to create richer and better content with what you've learned.

eBooks

eBooks (also written as Ebooks) are digital copies of a book, but because they are online they can be downloaded and read on a device such as a smartphone or tablet. They can be any length from 10 to 200 pages, and are typically written to solve a problem for a target audience. For marketing purposes, they are usually on the shorter side. They often have interesting graphics and images; some even have video and audio embedded into them. Because of that, sometimes they are referred to as "infotainment," as the ones that are done well are informational, as well as visually appealing. Those that are sold are typically less expensive than regular books, although for client attraction purposes, most are free. In order to access them, there is often a lead generation form requiring the interested party to provide an email address before downloading the eBook, which, of course, is valuable for marketing to that person at a later time.

As an example of successful eBook projects, lawyers Stephen Futeral and Thomas Nelson from Futeral & Nelson in Charleston have published several free eBooks on DUI, divorce, and gun laws in South Carolina. They offer them on their website as downloads, as well as through the iTunes®® Bookstore, and they promote them on their social media platforms. These lawyers are providing useful information to their target clients and, at the same time, positioning themselves as thought leaders, essentially THE lawyers to go to for those types of legal matters. The eBooks contain photos of them and contact information, strategically placed within the content to provide the opportunity for the potential client to reach out to them when needed.

eBooks are excellent content pieces that can be leveraged in many different ways. Content from the book can be used for your webinars, email campaigns social posting calendar, and on and on. Another advantage is that they can have a fairly long shelf life – at least a couple of years in most cases. Some authors increase their exposure even further by offering their eBooks on Amazon, iTunes® and various eReader marketplaces. Many eBook authors also go on to have full calendars of speaking engagements.

How to Create It

eBooks, such as those mentioned above that are designed primarily for client attraction purposes, tend to be shorter and easier to create and publish than a more traditional book. When creating your eBook, consider this formula for success:

- Lead generating eBooks should contain information your target clients need or want. Have you written a series of blogs on a particular topic that was well received? If so, you might think about compiling these together and creating a larger content piece covering the single topic, and publishing this as a single eBook. Perhaps you receive numerous questions around the same topic. The same concept applies, and you can use these Q & A's as the basis of your eBook.
- The title should be informative and enticing.
- Create an outline of how you'll address the main points you want to include so that your eBook is organized and flows well.
- Use a cover and eBook template for your eBooks, including interesting visuals and graphics if available that are designed by your

marketing department or a freelance designer. Some creative people have even used Microsoft Word or PowerPoint to create an eBook template. The important point here is that all of your eBooks should look the same in order to reinforce your brand.

- Break complex topics down into subsections with subtitles that are easy to scan, again to help the flow of the content.
- Incorporate call outs or emphasis boxes to highlight important takeaways.
- Include links to other relevant content you have created, or third-party sources of related content.
- Make sure to hire someone to read and edit it for you. There are many options available for hiring inexpensive editors, including many "for hire" type websites, such as Craigslist, Upwork, and Elance.
- Make it easy for readers to share your eBook on social media by incorporating share buttons for the various social media platforms within the eBook itself.
- Have your web designer add a code to your eBook landing page where people download it, in order to collect analytics. Google Analytics is one excellent free option. This will allow you to see how many people have downloaded your eBook, where they come from, and other statistics.
- Publish it as a high resolution PDF. Upload it on your website and get ready to share the link.

Find as many ways as possible to promote it and even consider giving it away for the small price of a completed lead form from the potential client. eBooks are the type of content that can be created once and can then go quite a long way to building your book of business.

Infographics

Infographics, or more literally "information – graphics," are visually interesting presentations of information and a very popular way of relaying information online. Rather than a simple list or set of bullets to convey information, an infographic combines data and good design to tell a story, with the goal to influence a reader to stop and pause while they take in the information you are sharing.

Infographics are valuable for communicating statistics, research results, how-to information, and tips. The most popular ones tend to cover topics in health, business, careers, general knowledge, education, current events, food, entertainment, and sports. There are even infographics about infographics.

Infographics are part of what's known as visual marketing, which is an effective way to get your message across succinctly. Besides being creative and memorable, the power of infographics is that they contain links to the creator's website, otherwise known as backlinks. When people share them with their networks and others post them on their websites, it drives traffic back to the linked website.

Adding the use of infographics into your content can help elevate your brand, representing you and your firm as "socially savvy" and yourself as a content marketer who is using the most relevant and current tools. Another benefit of using infographics is that they help to improve your search engine rankings when users look for information on a related topic, as infographics tend to get a lot of "natural" sharing because they are interesting to most readers.

Unless you have a knack for graphic design, I recommend you have a graphic designer create your infographics. But there will be some direction needed from you with respect to the content. First, look for and identify a topic that you feel your potential clients are really interested in, be it the issue that "everyone" is talking about in your area of focus or simply something you know can be interesting and of value at the same time. To give you an idea, one of the popular infographics available in 2014 according to BuzzSumo is titled "Rights You Have When Interacting With a Police Officer."[34]

Do some research using platforms such as Google News or Google Trends to look at topics that are trending on the web that could potentially line up with your area of expertise. For ideas, review other infographics that have been popular and performed well on other platforms, such as Pinterest or Visual.ly.

Next, collect the information you'll use in the infographic. Remember, it can represent any set of data that you want it to, including hard statistics, tips and tricks, or somewhere in between the two. Once you've gathered the information, it's time to bring in the designer. Relay the salient points that you want to get across to the reader and reveal the "takeaway" point of the entire infographic. Ask the graphic designer to provide suggestions about the best way to portray this message in an impactful way. Keep the design simple, yet interesting, using minimal text and imagery to get the best result.

No matter who designs your infographic, make sure to step back from it once it's created and evaluate it. Is it impactful? Does it tell a story or make a compelling argument? Make sure to use the best quality photography or graphics available to you, as you want to ensure that the infographic will hold up as it is shared, reposted, and spread on the web. Also attribute information to your sources where applicable, as it lends credibility and perceived value to the data you're sharing. Last, make sure it has a link back to your website.

White Papers

White papers are typically 2-10 page guides or reports designed to help a reader understand a topic, explain trends, navigate a problem, or provide information on how to use a product or service. They often include statistics, research findings, survey results, bulleted lists, and may incorporate graphics. They can be good pieces of content to explain a complicated or often misunderstood issue. You should know that white papers and eBooks are often terms that are used interchangeably, especially when referring to shorter eBooks.

The firm Latham & Watkins uses white papers effectively. An example is a white paper geared to existing clients called "Top 10 Things to Know About President Obama's Cuba-Related Announcement," which was published after the President's announcement regarding American-Cuban relations.[35] It was authored by seven lawyers at the firm and at the end, suggests readers who have questions or want further explanation should contact one of those lawyers. In a section called "You Might Also Be Interested In," they cross promote other content, including the firm's webcasts.

Clearly, this firm's lawyers understand how to position themselves as thought leaders and how to build top of mind awareness with their clients. The white papers can also influence potential clients by demonstrating the firm's lawyers are informed on what is current and share their knowledge in a timely fashion with their clients. Ideally, this type of timely content may even cause potential clients to question their own lawyers and how valuable they are to them.

One approach is to collaborate with another attorney or service provider, focusing on a topic that is helpful to either your target or existing clients. Effective white papers are solid in substance, not "salesey," and often are purely educational. Once a reader has absorbed the great information you've provided and decided you are the right lawyer for them, they will use your authorship information to find out more about you and how to contact you. One of the best attributes of white papers is that they sell you in a non-threatening way, as you're seen as a trusted resource offering needed information, rather than a hard-selling sales pitch.

When writing it, whether you're providing insight about a change in the law or explaining a complex topic like environmental issues, remember to focus on the client's potential questions and needs. What are their pain points or challenges? How can you or your firm help? In what way can your firm help the reader achieve his or her goals? How have you approached similar issues in the past?

Be professional in your writing style, but as mentioned when I discussed your voice, make sure to come across as approachable and create a tone that makes the reader feel like they could sit across the table from you and feel comfortable.

Add graphics, bullet points, and strong attention-grabbing titles and headlines. Ultimately, make the white paper inviting so users will want to read it and reach out to you.

Case Studies

A case study or customer success story profiles a good result for a client or customer and highlights how a company, or in this case a firm, helped obtain a positive outcome. They are usually one to two pages and contain the challenge, objectives, solution, and results achieved. For marketing purposes, they often contain a testimonial from the satisfied client. Some companies are now using video case studies with the same kind of information, which can be easily adaptable for the legal industry, as well.

The purpose of a case study is to establish credibility by telling a story about how you and your firm helped solve a problem. Good case studies are written with the potential client in mind. By the time the person finishes reading about the solution you provided, they can imagine themselves getting the same types of results by working with you. Case studies allow a lawyer or firm to go in depth into the various qualities and advantages of their services and expertise.

Compelling case studies are like a drama. There is often a main character so a reader can relate to a person and his or her challenge. The more detail you're able to include the better, assuming you have obtained your client's permission. The problem or villain is clearly described so the reader cares about the outcome, and the service provider saves the day with their expertise, strategy, and solution. Use adjectives to create feelings about the whole situation. Describe the results, the impact, and what it all has meant for the main character.

The problem you choose to profile in a case study should be one that is relevant to the target clients you are trying to attract. This type of content can be used in a variety of places, so make sure to create a call to action to be included, such as, "If you're having a similar problem, contact our offices for a consultation," and then provide the relevant links and information. Don't forget to include photos, if relevant. Client success stories don't have to be just copy. They instead can be what we call a pillar piece of content that has other variations of the same thing – video, podcast, or a SlideShare presentation. They can be hosted on your website, as well as shared via social channels, thus adding mileage to a simple case study far beyond its short success story.

FAQs

"Frequently Asked Questions" or FAQs can influence a target client by showcasing your subject matter authority and demonstrating that you understand your clients' needs. Few people consider crafting FAQs, yet they are quite valuable for several reasons:

- FAQs address commonly asked questions which can cut down the time you spend answering the same questions over and over with potential clients
- FAQs can instill trust by providing helpful information before someone has ever stepped into your office
- If questions are included that people are often uncomfortable asking, FAQs remove a barrier that might stop a client from contacting you

If you're creating FAQs, include questions people *should* be asking, but don't know enough to ask. Keep the answers simple and to the point and avoid sales or marketing speak at all costs. If it's a complex topic, consider breaking the issue at hand into sections. Have your web developer incorporate share functionality on your website FAQs to enable easy dissemination of your content. Also, consider creating video version of FAQs that have the added benefit of potential clients seeing you in the video and building trust with them, allowing them a stronger comfort level to contact you. Remember to include statements that ask, "Do you have a question that isn't answered here?" The feedback might give you insight into adding more questions and answers.

Press Releases

You have heard of a press release, which up until recent years was the way to communicate with news media in the hopes of getting their attention to print or broadcast a story. It used to be that the only way you could make an announcement and inform a large audience was through a newspaper, radio, or TV station. Today, this is no longer the case and the media is no longer needed as a filter to "broadcast" your message. With digital options available to everyone, you are your own publisher. You can write and distribute press releases on your own using a newswire, which can lead to numerous entities sharing your release on their respective websites and even via social media.

As a former journalist, here's my take on what you need to know about news releases. There are essentially two main strategies. The first is geared toward getting a reporter's attention. Let me tell you that journalists, editors, and producers are inundated with press releases because, as mentioned, anyone can write and publish them today. Due to the fact that so many people are issuing releases, it's actually a lot harder to get a reporter's attention today than it was just a few years ago using only a press release.

Besides the sheer volume of releases, journalists and newsroom editors have set criteria about what they'll cover, and more often than not, your press release will not warrant their attention. They have to consider their own target audience, which is likely much broader than your target audience of potential clients.

Your press release is competing with all kinds of potential stories—celebrity gossip, crime, controversies, political shenanigans, llamas on the loose, and other salacious headlines. The decision makers in newsrooms will evaluate the story you're proposing in your release and judge it, deciding if it is compelling enough to entice their readers or audience to want to know the story. I often tell our company's clients that just because you think the public should know something important doesn't mean newsroom producers or editors will think it will generate ratings or readership.

There are a few lawyers who have figured out how to get media attention consistently, Gloria Allred being one of them. She and her firm follow the news, quite literally. They seem to find and attract victims to represent who are linked to high-profile cases. They issue news alerts and press releases and hold press briefings that garner decent media attention for their firm and its lawyers.

Others have obtained press coverage due to wins in criminal cases that have captured the public's attention. On several occasions when I was a reporter, lawyers representing medical malpractice victims or people affected by scams alerted me. Their clients' experiences made for compelling stories, and I reported on them. In all of these instances, the story involving the lawyer had a large audience appeal.

The second way lawyers typically get a reporter's attention is when their story is of interest to what we call niche media. This would include topics covered by a business broadcast, health show, or in a financial column. Even if you have a story that might be of interest, a press release is usually not enough to gain publication. There's often a pitching and media relations strategy that PR and communications pros understand is needed in order to get on a reporter's radar and have them take the next step.

Here's the secret—most lawyers don't need highly publicized stories or news media to achieve their client attraction goals. You still want to use press releases, but rather than focus on news media, focus on your target clients. You can use news releases and digital distribution strategies to reach clients looking for your services, in a targeted manner and quite effectively, using the SEO (Search Engine Optimization) strategy for press releases. (See the section on SEO in the chapter How to Decide What Types of Content to Create for more information.)

Here's how it works. You write a press release and use a newswire to distribute it such as PR Newswire. Then you can select distribution categories based on industries and markets. For example, let's say your business objective is to get more tech entrepreneurs in the Bay Area as clients. The steps you would take are:

1. Publish a case study about an intellectual property case in Silicon Valley.
2. Issue a press release using a newswire targeted to the tech and business industries in the Northern California region about the release of the case study.
3. Include links back to your website in the press release.

Media entities, bloggers, and other online content sites focused on tech will likely carry your press release because they need fresh content on their web pages. They might even tweet out links to your press release. Sprinkled over the Internet, that provides a decent amount of links back to your website.

Be sure to allow social sharing of it, and don't forget about hosting it on your website. In the hypothetical scenario, this would help your website rank higher for the topic about intellectual property in Silicon Valley. When a potential client is searching for intellectual property information or legal guidance, since your site has a decent ranking for those terms, there's a higher likelihood that someone who needs help with this will land on your website or your press release. They have now discovered you when they didn't even know your name, and it may well be at midnight when you're nice and cozy in bed.

It's also possible a tech blogger with a decent following may see the release and either incorporate it into her blog, or she may even reach out to you to get more information in order to write a blog post. The audience following her blog, though niche, has more potential clients for you making it therefore advantageous to be in "front of" her followers, rather than the broader audience on the local TV station. For a variety of reasons, well-written press releases can be a good direct-to-client marketing option that doesn't even involve the media.

Another strategy is to identify something newsworthy to announce. Did the firm have a big win or settlement? Did one of your clients have a breakthrough or have they filed a precedent setting lawsuit? Have you or someone on your team received new certifications or something worth promoting? Have you published a new white paper or eBook? What about legal or community awards? Are there any seminars or events you'll be hosting for the public or your peers? Has someone on your team been nominated to a board or had any special achievements? All of these and more are topics for potential releases.

Once you've chosen your topic, how do you actually write the release? Here's the anatomy of a press release:

Anatomy of the Press Release

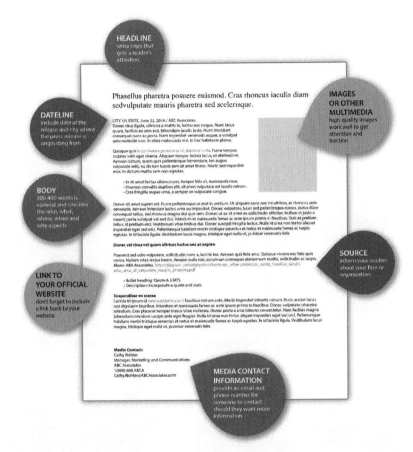

Many individuals attempting to use press releases in their strategy make some critical errors. From the onset, keep in mind that you are trying to engage your target clients, editors, journalists, and even bloggers. Within 10-20 seconds, many editors make a decision to continue reading or move on to the next piece in search of the content they will cover in their news publication or on their channel. How will you get and keep their attention in order to make the cut?

Here are some basic rules to make sure your press release doesn't fall into the "deleted" file too quickly:

1. Write a headline that will want people to read it, and even better, tweet it.
2. Make sure you date the release and mention the location or place it's taking place in or the city where your firm is based. The typical format would be: "Dallas, Texas – July 10, 2015. XYZ Legal Firm, specializing in patent law, announces…etc."
3. The first paragraph is critical and will influence others to keep reading, or not. Include the 5 W's - who, what, where, when and why information.
4. The second paragraph (and third if you have room) should provide more detail and consider including a quote from a relevant person. Make your best effort to keep the message easy to grasp.
5. Include high quality photos, charts or links to video to support the message of the press release.
6. Title your press release as such when distributing it and sharing it. In other words, make sure to call your press release a press release in the email used to distribute it, in the title of the release and even in the message to the press.
7. Be sure to include your firm information and, of course, your contact information.
8. Include targeted keywords throughout the press release, including terms that are important to both your target clients and the publications in which you are trying to get published.

So who should receive your press releases? Besides using a newswire distribution, send them to everyone in your email newsletter database, as well as your current clients. Send it also to any reporters, writers of publications that are geared to your target clients, and bloggers who focus on a relevant topic with whom you have a relationship. Overall, the press release is a strong element in your content strategy that can be leveraged in many different ways.

To get started, download our tip sheet, How to Write a Press Release.

To download the How to Write a Press Release Tip Sheet go to www. MicheleRuiz.com/ContentMarketingResources.

Emails and Newsletters

At this point in your career, you obviously know what emails are and have likely seen more email newsletters than you have time to read. You also have a few that you read each time they hit your inbox. Why those? It's most likely because they're relevant to you and you find the content to be of value. You likely trust the quality of the information in the newsletter and like the tone in which it's written, the sender's communication style and perhaps even the way it looks or is designed.

Lawyers and legal firms that use email marketing successfully find it to be a particularly beneficial tool for client retention and referrals. Have you considered all the ways an email can be used for content marketing? For example, if your area of expertise is the health industry and your clients are hospitals, a client-centric email marketing strategy can be very useful. Start with a blog on your website highlighting a challenge in the industry and ways you can help clients deal with the issues arising out of it. From there, use your email newsletter to highlight the topic of the blog post with a concise summary and include a link back to the blog so readers can go to it and read more.

The email newsletter is a great tool to share links to your content and drive readers to other communication channels in order to spread your message. In this example, you're helping to inform your clients about issues that can impact them, and in so doing, reminding your clients of the value you provide. You'll likely attract new potential clients to use your services. This is also an easy way for your clients to send more clients to you – simply by forwarding your email newsletter on to whomever they believe might benefit from its content.

When you consider that existing and prospective clients both expect you'll be communicating via email, and that by signing up for your news-letter, they've given you permission to contact them, an email marketing strategy that pushes information directly to your target audiences can be very beneficial. This process will keep you engaged with your current clients even if you don't happen to be working with them on a matter at that particular time. Likewise, a constant email touchpoint strategy for your potential clients ensures that your name comes to the forefront when a need arises.

Email marketing has some distinct advantages. The available email marketing platforms and solutions provide data and analytics, measuring how many emails are opened, how many people click on any links within the email, who and how many have unsubscribed, and how many emails "bounce back" because of a bad email address or spam filters. These metrics can give you important insights into the effectiveness of your messaging and your strategy, allowing for optimizations to improve performance at a granular level and provide a strong return on investment.

Here are some of the main elements of a good email marketing strategy and what you'll need to consider as you get started:

- Decide if it's the right strategy for your existing and target clients. If you have a volume-based practice where you need to find a constant stream of new clients, then other content strategies such as blogging and videos may be a better use of your limited time.
- Be clear on why you're implementing an email marketing strategy so your messaging and content choices within the emails are in alignment with your objectives.
- Use one of the email marketing solutions (most of which are reasonably priced), such as MailChimp™, Constant Contact™, or AWeber™, that have templates, analytics, and easy-to-use dashboards. These solutions automate part of the process for you. They also have opt-in sign up forms as part of their templates so you don't violate the federal CAN-SPAM Act.
- If you're not the creative type, it's worth hiring a graphic designer for a few hours to design the layout of your email newsletter template so it represents your brand well.
- Determine the types of content you'll be promoting within your newsletter and make sure it all ties back to your overall objectives and is relevant to your target audiences.
- Establish how often your email newsletters will be sent out, taking into consideration what it will take to put the content together so you can add it to your marketing workflow. There's no hard and fast rule other than consistency and a frequency your clients can rely on.

It's important to be likeable and avoid the mistakes that make people dislike either you or your email marketing. When collecting potential clients' information, be sure to always have a "yes, send me information about your firm, news, and events" button that can be checked by the potential client, giving you permission to communicate with them about your services and news you want to share. Ask them at the same time if they prefer text or HTML emails, allowing you to send the emails to your readers in the way they each most prefer.

The subject line of the email is critical. Be sure to avoid hype and vagueness. Make sure it sets expectations for recipients about exactly what the email will be about, rather than a vague "Weekly Newsletter" subject. This is your first impression with the recipient and an opportunity to make them engage with your content. Make the subject line compelling, short, and "open worthy" in the mind of your target audience. Remember, the first hurdle is to get them to open the email, so take time to make a subject line that drives the wanted behavior.

Now, it's time to review the body of the email. Make the email personal by using the subscriber's name in the greeting. Write it in a way that makes it seem you are communicating directly with that person, versus covering a whole group of people with a shotgun approach.

The design should be simple and clean, and it should get your message across to the recipient without being too confusing or convoluted. Remember to think about the mobile user who opens emails on smartphones or tablets and be sure your design will work well for both. Make the email creative, including relevant images, if available. Note, however, that some email systems block emails with photos, so avoid inserting one big image for the content of your email.

You can add links to videos, as well, making the content even more engaging. If you have them, include links to your site or a targeted landing page throughout the email, rather than just at the end, to improve the chance the user will click on your link.

Be sure the message or information you're sharing is relevant to the group you are mailing to. Don't send information on new probate tax laws to a potential client interested in real estate leases. By keeping the content relevant to your client and their needs, you are showing respect for the relationship and decreasing the likelihood of them unsubscribing.

Keep in mind that people want to get to the meat of the email content right away. Avoid trying to educate a reader with a long explanation within the email newsletter. It's better to give a brief summary and lead them to some other site (your website, blog, SlideShare, etc.) with links to dive in deeper if they so choose.

If you're promoting other content, such as a white paper or webinar, keep the calls to action (CTAs) focused solely to one item within an email. For example, in one email, only insert a CTA to download the white paper. Promote signing up for a webinar in a separate email, so you won't overload the recipient with too much and lessen their urge to take the next step. Overall, email marketing can be a strategy that provides a good return on your efforts. Think about sharing client results, news about partners and associates, recognitions and press coverage, and even holiday messages. Some law firms implement a client-centric strategy and share insights about changes in laws or promote information blogs or webinars being offered.

Others build a reputation as a provider of good information by curating other people's content (known as OPC) such as articles, blogs, and videos, and then provide their own opinions and observations. I share more about OPC in the next section.

One last note – email fatigue is a challenge you need to be mindful of when implementing a newsletter strategy. It takes concerted effort, creativity, and tweaking to get impactful results. I recommend you consult with an email marketing expert to go over the analytics once you've begun, in order to guide you in determining how to make improvements. For example, if you make changes to your messaging, design, and layout, the schedule for when you send it out, or even the subject lines, you could improve the effectiveness of your strategy with each change. A well-thought-out plan with some testing or optimization can grow your client base and increase revenue.

Other People's Content

While ideally you are creating some of your own content, it is quite common to augment your content marketing strategy by sharing content others have created, as well. This is known as other people's content or OPC. Your goal is to be helpful to your client base, so the key here is to share quality content that you have no trouble being associated with. It should align with your business objectives and be relevant to your target clients. As long as the content meets that criteria, think about what they want to learn more about and the information they're seeking online. As long as the informative content accomplishes those goals, then you are still creating value, regardless of the original source of the content you are sharing.

Some people put up content for discussion, as well. It might be a news story, where the sharer asks her followers what their opinion is on the subject. She may or may not agree with the gist of the story but is sharing it and eliciting engagement. As I've covered earlier, the more engagement on your social profiles, the more people will see what you post. Because of this, I strongly recommend implementing a content-sharing strategy. Here's why:

- Saves time and resources by not having to create a lot of content
- Grows relationship with other people online
- You get a halo effect from highlighting other experts
- Fills your posting calendar, and keeps you top-of-mind
- Helps with content ratio so not everything you're putting out is about you and your brand
- Contributes to building your overall following
- It makes those recipients of your sharing generosity more likely to share yours in return
- Reinforces you're "in the know" and in the right circles
- Positions you as a "giver" and, in this case, a giver of helpful content for your target audience, no matter where it comes from

Social media guru Guy Kawasaki says there are two components to his content-sharing strategy. In an interview he gave to *Social Media Examiner* he says the most important test is what he calls the "reshare test."[36] "Are you sharing something that other people will share with their friends and followers?" he asked. In this context, I would add one more group – their peers.

The other component he mentions is that sharing content is a key indicator. With a share, you risk your reputation. So, whatever you share should match your brand promise that you've developed and what you stand for.

8 Content Inventory and Assessment

As part of getting ready to create your online content, it's worthwhile to assess what content you may already have – brochures, PowerPoint presentations, videos, digital assets, content you've shared on your website, and anything else. Going through the process of inventorying what exists and what you have to work with can save you time and money. You may find some of the content you already have can be leveraged and may only need a "refresh" to be used as part of your overall content-marketing strategy.

Start by creating a spreadsheet with the following columns:

- Tracking ID Number (create an ID for every document, presentation, photo, video, etc.)
- Name of Document / Page Title if on Web
- Date Content Created
- Web Address
- Document Type (brochure, speech, web page, PDF, Word, video, PowerPoint, etc.)
- Location of Content (where it is stored both offline and online and if on a computer or drive)
- Target Audience (who the content was created for)
- Purpose (presentation, marketing, branding, PR, etc.)

With my company's corporate clients, we ask the people who create or use content to lay out every hard copy piece of content on a conference room table, and we start by numbering them and filling out a spreadsheet. We then go through every digital asset, followed by content shared on their websites and inventory those, too. Last, we include content created by others that includes our clients' expertise (i.e. articles, opinion pieces, blogs, etc.) and track that, as well.

The next step is assessing the value of the existing content for the marketing strategy. This includes the following:

- Business objective - Does the content support a business objective?
- Client centric - Is the content client centric or is it pure "selling" content? Does the content address a need? If it's focused on your clients' pain points, it's good content, or at least can be the basis of good content with some adjustments.
- Buying cycle - What client decision point is the content best used for? Assuming it can be used, where in the buying cycle is it best suited?
- Quality – Is it well written, crafted, and edited, or does it need improvement? Is it easy to understand? Is it outdated?
- "Shareability" and Likeableness – Is the content in a format or designed in a way that will influence people to share it or like it online?
- Brand alignment – Is the content's branding and look and feel consistent with your firm's branding? Is it outdated?
- SEO – If the content is on a website, is it designed well for SEO? Is there good use of keywords and headings?
- Raw content usability - This can be items like speeches on a Word document, videos of a presentation, or photos. Can the raw content be created into something valuable?
- Pillar content value –This is when the words or key points in a comprehensive piece of content can be repurposed into another kind of content. For example, a PowerPoint used in a presentation has key insights that can be incorporated into a blog.
- Calls to Action – Does the content contain CTAs and, if so, are they strong and still relevant?

Take the spreadsheet used to inventory content and now add these points above as additional columns. See below. When assessing the quality and usability of existing content, give it a score.

	A	B	C	D	E	F	G	H	I	J	K	L	M	N	O
	Tracking ID Number	Name of Document / Page title if on Web	Date Content Created	Web Address - URL (if applicable)	Document Type	Location of Content	Target Audience	Purpose	Notes	Business Objectives - Does the content support a business objective?	Quality of content Score (clientcentric, overall quality, shareability and likeability, brand alignment) 1 means use as is; 2 means with changes can be used; 3 means not usable	SEO (if applicable)	Raw content usability – can the raw content be created into something valuable or another piece of content?	Pillar Content Value	CTAs (Calls to Action) Does the content contain CTAs and if so, are they strong and still relevant?
1															
2															
3															
4															

- 1 means it is in great shape to use as is
- 2 means with some modifications it can be used
- 3 means it's not a fit for your content marketing strategy

Visit my website to download a version of this spreadsheet to help you inventory and assess your existing content. I recommend tracking any new content created, as well as conducting a periodic review of your items to make sure all are still great pieces of content.

> To download the Content Inventory Spreadsheet go to www.MicheleRuiz.com/ContentMarketingResources.

9 How to Decide What Types of Content to Create

The decision about the types of content to create for your target clients, their influencers, and your current clients in order to stay top of mind for them is driven by the following key factors:

- Your overall resources, in terms of money and time
- The prime ways your target audiences like to receive information
- SEO to pull target audiences back to your website (either your firm's or your own)
- Best types of content for each decision point in the typical buying process for your services

The first two factors we've covered earlier in the book, so here, we'll discuss the decision points in a typical buying process and go further into SEO.

If you think about how someone who doesn't know of you ultimately makes a decision to contact you, you may realize there are steps to gaining their trust. These steps can be broken down as follows:

Decision Stages in the Buying Process

| KNOW NOTHING ABOUT YOU | KNOW SOMETHING ABOUT YOU | INTERESTED IN WHAT YOU HAVE TO OFFER | COMPARE YOU TO OTHER OPTIONS | TAKE THE DESIRED ACTION |

KNOW NOTHING ABOUT YOU: Online it all starts with a search engine. A potential client enters words into a search bar, looking for information to answer a question or solve a pain point, and that is often the beginning of the buying process. Content focused on pain points or challenges is ideal at this stage to get their attention. Remember that at this juncture, clients don't care so much about your services. They care about themselves and their problems or challenges. So this is the "creating awareness about you" stage.

KNOW SOMETHING ABOUT YOU: Once they've landed on your content that is focused on their needs, they now know something about you. But it doesn't mean they are yet convinced you are the right lawyer for them. This is the stage at which content that communicates "this is how it should be done" or that conveys that you are adept at helping with the issues the client is dealing with will help you stand out.

INTERESTED IN WHAT YOU HAVE TO OFFER: Once they have found your useful content relevant to their challenges, they are persuaded you are an expert who can help them. This is the point at which they are interested in what you have to offer. At this stage, content that informs the user of your successes and your potential solutions, further supported by client testimonials, becomes compelling.

COMPARE YOU TO OTHER OPTIONS: Now the potential client is convinced that you are competent and they could use your professional legal services. Often, the next decision point is comparing you to other lawyers. Content that persuades them you are the right person to contact versus another lawyer is key. This is where your unique value proposition becomes really important and could be a tipping point in your favor. Refer back to the section about client attraction value proposition in Chapter 5 if you need a refresher on this.

TAKE THE DESIRED ACTION: Several types of content that address all of these stages with specific calls to action, such as to visit your website, have a higher likelihood to persuade a potential client to contact you.

While some users may skip certain decision points before they consider reaching out, the best strategy is to create content that is well suited to each stage. In a good content marketing strategy, each piece of content individually drives to content in other stages of the buying process, therefore guiding the user along the purchase path.

Even if a potential client is referred to you by someone they know, there is a high probability they will go online to learn more about you and do their due diligence. Valuable content for each of the decision points is an opportunity to connect with your potential clients and allow them to rest easy in their decision to reach out to you.

Most people who implement a content marketing strategy focus on content at the first stage of this process, and completely ignore the later, equally important, decision points. Creating compelling content that supports the entire buying process is another way you can stand out from other lawyers.

Here's an example of a content plan that could work at each point of the buying process for a real estate lawyer we'll call Brian, whose clients buy and develop commercial property.

Buying Cycle Content Development Plan

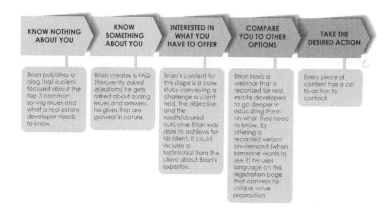

Notice that content at each decision point not only provides an opportunity for Brian to connect with potential clients, but also to gain more of their trust draw them to him. Each piece of content should promote the content offered at later stages, which further reinforces his expertise and the perception that he's the ideal real estate lawyer to fulfill the needs of commercial real estate developers.

In the content plan above, the assumptions are that Brian has reviewed his resources and decided he is publishing a blog as his core content type, with posts once a week. He feels he can comfortably manage this schedule based on his resources (i.e., time, bandwidth, his assistant's time). He's hiring a graphic designer to assist with creating one FAQ document and one case study focused on zoning issues. He decides to host both on his website, as they are good types of content for his clients who buy and develop commercial property. These content pieces along with his blog posts are good for SEO in order to pull people back to his website. Last, he's hosting and recording one webinar to provide deeper engagement with his target clients and top types of referrers. He records the webinar, which means he spends the time preparing it, the slide presentation, and the handout the attendees will receive only once. The webinar, however, is viewable repeatedly and on-demand by as many people who sign up for it.

Much like in Brian's scenario, deciding what content types you should focus on creating and publishing depends on your resources and the top ways your target clients like to get their information. After reviewing Chapter 7 and looking at the different types of content options, start your efforts by focusing on one or two types. For some clients, you may decide that video is preferable say, over case studies. In other instances, blogs and case studies may be better. The key is not to feel you should be creating all types of content, especially at the beginning, but rather the types that you feel will resonate most with your ideal clients. Once you've started, I recommend you get into a production and publishing groove before you expand into other content types.

Struggling for content ideas? No problem. Go to my website for my 25 content ideas for a quick start.

> To access the 25 Content Ideas to Get You Started go to
> www.MicheleRuiz.com/ContentMarketingResources.

SEO and Content

Content and SEO go together like bread and butter. When developing your online content, it is very important to look through the lens of SEO. Keywords, or terms that you feel are important words your clients might use to find you on the Internet, should be taken into consideration in order to launch an effective content marketing strategy. To maximize the return on your investment, it's critical to incorporate SEO strategies to pull people back to your website as covered earlier. Keyword strategies are a main part of SEO.

An ideal keyword strategy builds content around (1) your field of law, (2) those terms that match your area of expertise, (3) the keywords associated with the pain points you plan to address in your content, and (4) your target audience.

Ideal Keyword Strategy

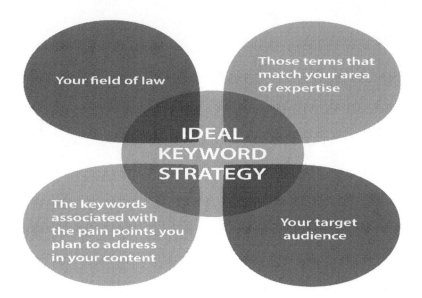

A website with lots of content using keywords in titles, headlines, and in the copy will significantly help increase rank to the top of the search engines.

For Brian, our fictional commercial real estate lawyer, the top keywords he would focus on revolve around the type of lawyer he is, the area of specialty he's focusing on (zoning), keywords associated with his client's pain points around zoning, and words used by his target clients who are the buyers and developers of commercial property. The best way to come up with potential keywords and keyword phrases is by conducting a keyword search. Keywords can be found using several tools, including AdWords Keyword Planner by Google. (New tools pop up frequently so do a search for "Keyword Tools" if you want other options.)

Start by thinking of terms that are relevant to your area of expertise. Insert the keyword phrase someone would most likely type into a search engine, and the online keyword tools will populate a list of search terms and how frequently they are searched per month.

Below is an example of some of the keywords and keyword phrases that came up in a search to be used by Brian. It is a limited list of keywords for his field of law, area of expertise, target clients and their pain points that people really search for.

There could be others. Consider various spellings of terms also, such as swing set vs. swingset.

Brian has a goal for his firm's website to become a one-stop shop for all legal needs and information regarding commercial zoning. In essence, he would like it to become an encyclopedia for commercial zoning information. His quality content – blog posts, FAQs, case studies, webinars – collectively will be *the* place his potential clients will visit when they have questions related to this issue. Relevant keywords play an important role in deciding the focus of his content marketing strategy.

In doing keyword searches, those with the highest search rank indicate they are the more competitive phrases. If you were buying paid search advertising, it would mean they would be the most expensive. In terms of content, it means it could be more difficult for your blogs, videos, etc., to rank high on search engines, compared to lesser searched terms, due to the competition (both in paid advertising and in content) using those keywords.

Specificity or using tightly targeted terms is the secret to your content being found and for attracting the right types of people to your content. For example, broad terms such as *"lawyers"* or *"attorneys"* are the most searched and most competitive. In Brian's zoning example, *"real estate law"* and *"real estate lawyer,"* as well as *"commercial real estate"* and *"commercial real estate investing"* are highly searched, compared to *"commercial real estate lawyer,"* *"real estate zoning lawyer,"* and *"land use attorney."* Building content around the terms *"lawyers"* and *"attorneys"* would be less effective than the terms *"real estate zoning lawyer"* or even the more searched phrase *"real estate lawyer."*

VARIANCE 135,000

ZONING REGULATIONS 590

ZONING ISSUES 70

Zoning Ordinance 1600

ZONING 14,800

Conditional use permit 1,000

Zoning Laws 2400

COMMERCIAL ZONING 210

Zoning Problems 10

Looking at keywords for pain points geared to Brian's target clients, we see that the broad term "*zoning*" is a highly searched word with over 14,000 searches per month. "*Zoning laws,*" "*zoning ordinance*" and "*commercial zoning*" are very specific and searched less often—in some instances, as few as 200 searches per month. Enough people are searching using those lower volume terms taken in the aggregate, yet there may not be a lot of content available that includes those words. Therefore, Brian's content, by incorporating those targeted phrases, has a higher chance of surfacing near the top of the search engine results.

What does this all mean? First, you need to know what people are searching for so you can create content using those words and phrases, making it easy for your audience to find your content. It would be a waste to create blogs with titles and keywords within them that no one is searching for. If you are creating good quality content around topics people want to know about, then using specific keywords increases the chances it will be shared – both by email and social media. This is what we call "shareable content," and ultimately that's what you want.

Also, terms that are too broad are not as effective as using more specific terms. While, generally speaking, these more specific terms are searched less, chances are the more specific the term, the more relevant it will be to the audience landing on your content and going to your website. It's better to have 75 relevant people (potential clients) finding your content per month than 900 people, of which very few are your target clients. If you think about how many clients you want to bring in to grow your book of business over the next year, you can see that it's not about quantity of visitors, but rather, it's about driving relevant website traffic.

This is not to say you shouldn't create some content using some of the broader terms, but only as part of a strategy where lesser- searched keyword phrases are incorporated, as well.

Keyword sections for SEO and content marketing should be used for your planned content as part of your content calendar. Before someone writes an article, describes a service, or creates a blog post, considering keyword possibilities is a winning strategy.

There is more that can be done to drive traffic by bringing in SEO and website experts and going deeper into an SEO analysis and audit. For example:

- Analysis of how you're ranking for key terms and where you should be creating additional content. In Brian's example, if his website (and content) were ranking well for the keyword phrase "zoning issues," but not for others that are strategic for his target clients, then focusing on content using the other phrases would be a good step, rather than creating more blog posts around "zoning issues." This would open up a whole other group of people being pulled to his website.
- An SEO analysis of competitors and what keywords they are ranking for to develop a strategy leading to competitive advantage.
- Website usability and conversion analysis to ensure that the SEO traffic is paying off.

In the end, the importance of SEO can't be understated. You should consider SEO and keywords as part of your content marketing strategy, or you're not maximizing the opportunity for target clients to find you on the Internet.

10 Pulling a Content Marketing Strategy Together

In order to roll out a strategy that is effective and efficient, it is important to go through the steps outlined in this book leading up to this chapter. My strategic communications company, Ruiz Strategies, works with some of the largest corporations in the world, and this is the same process my team and I use as we develop and implement social media and content marketing strategies for those global companies.

To review, here are the main steps in the process covered in this book so far:

- Establish business goals and how you will know if you've achieved them
- Identify target clients and influencers and developed client personas for each one
- Develop your client attraction value proposition
- Determine where your client's are on social media
- Review your resources to implement your strategy
- Decide whether you are hosting your content, like blogs, on your firm's website or your own
- Inventory existing content and analyze it
- Analyze keywords and prioritize your keyword phrase strategy for SEO
- Consider the decision points in the buying process to plan content for each stage
- Choose what types of content you will create

You can go back to the Chapters 5, 8 and 9 for more details on these steps.

Marketing Path To Success

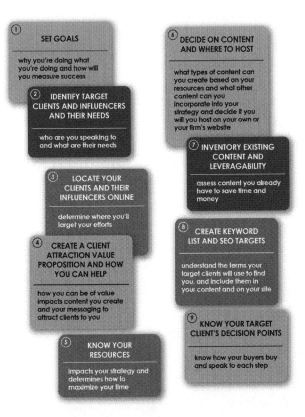

The graphic above describes the path you'll take as you develop your strategy and content. Follow these steps and you'll be on your way to a successful client attraction strategy to help you grow your book of business.

Why all of this before we have even started focusing on the specifics of a social media and content marketing strategy? Because most lawyers give up when they don't see clear results from all the effort they're putting in. More often than not, this is because they don't understand that in order for a strategy to be effective and worth the time invested, you need to be able to connect it back to your overall business objectives. Once you've taken that step, you can then focus on the ever-important content strategy. Many jump in by creating a social media profile without going through this process, then get frustrated and abandon the efforts. That is a mistake. By jumping in and then going silent, you are communicating something to your potential clients. And it's not a great message. In that situation, it would be better to not have jumped in at all. So if you've skipped the earlier chapters, I encourage you now to go back and take the time to read them. It will be worth it in the end.

Choosing the Channel: Finding Your Clients on the Web

Besides determining the types of content you will create, another key part of your strategy is deciding where you will distribute and promote that content online so that your target clients and their influencers will see it. In other words, you'll need to choose the most appropriate content marketing channels on the Internet for your audience. Deciding which core social media channels to use, i.e. LinkedIn, Twitter, Facebook, YouTube, etc., should primarily be based on what client personas you're focused on. Certain channels are better for particular types of potential clients and referrers than others. To review in detail the demographics of the social media platforms, see Chapter 6.

Many people make a critical mistake in this area, which results in an ineffective strategy. One should not start this process with deciding which social media platform or channel to use, but rather, by first defining the client persona(s). The next step is choosing the content that is best suited for achieving business objectives, and last, choosing the most appropriate social channel for that target client(s). Getting clear on your content strategy should drive the decision as to which core marketing channels to use.

The other factor to take into consideration when choosing a channel, is your depth of resources, most particularly the amount of time at your disposal to manage the platforms. If you're limited in time or people to help manage your channels, you should start by focusing on the top two channels best suited for your goals. It is better to be really engaged on two channels than doing a so-so job on four channels.

To demonstrate this, let's go back to Brian, our fictional commercial real estate attorney. His core content is a blog. His business objective is to bring in more clients who buy and develop commercial property, and he has built his content strategy to support his revenue targets. His resources, specifically people, are himself and his assistant, who together can devote at most a couple of hours a week.

His channels are LinkedIn and Twitter—LinkedIn because most real estate developers are users of this professional platform, and Twitter because of the sheer number of people using it, as well as the fact that it is an open platform, therefore, whatever is tweeted can come up as a search engine result.

To help you decide which channels make the most sense in letting your clients know about your content, refer to the Chapter 6 to learn about each channel and its demographics.

Contributing Your Content

Your content can be valuable to third-party sites that could use blogs and articles, while at the same time offering you additional exposure. Contributing content to other sources you don't own or control is called content syndication. The *Huffington* Post is a well-known site that relies substantially on other people's content. The benefit to the contributors is an audience they may not otherwise reach.

Trade publications, niche media properties, news media columns, business journals, and others will often consider article and/or blog submissions because they get content for free. If you think of your target audiences and influencers, there might be an opportunity to develop a content partnership where you submit your own quality blogs or videos to a relevant site.

Keep in mind that content syndication works only if it aligns with your business goals. Guest blogging for distribution in other publications (both on and offline) can take a lot of time, especially if you're creating custom content for a third party that you're not also hosting on your own website, which is often required. And remember, each article or blog you syndicate should offer the option to share a brief bio of you and link back to your website. Ideally, the demographics of the third-party site should align with the audience you're trying to reach.

Mapping Out the Strategy

In order to understand how to use the process to map out your strategy, let's look at a different scenario for an attorney, who I'll call Julie, who specializes in environmental law and whose target clients are businesses in California.

The following is a simple example using only one type of client and one of her business goals. Note that a fully fleshed out strategy should include this process for all goals, target clients, and influencers.

Example of Core Elements in Building Content Marketing Strategy

Business goals:	– increase revenue by 35% in 12 months	See chapter 5
Target clients' needs:	– business owners who grapple with environmental issues – need guidance in order to avoid potential violations – need to stay compliant with laws in order to operate – need help with complex legal issues – they can face litigation due to environmental disputes – their reputation can be affected from citizen opposition	See chapter 5
Target client demographics (client persona):	– located in California – annual revenue of $250,000 or more	See chapter 5
Client attraction value proposition:	*I help business owners save time, money, and aggravation by helping them navigate the complexities of California's environmental laws. I also help them avoid costly legal mistakes in their operations and documentation.*	See chapter 5
Resources for content marketing:	– people: me and my assistant; web master and SEO specialist, as needed – time: my time: 2 hours per week or 8 hours per month; assistant time: 2 hours per week or 8 hours per month – $1,000 per month for marketing costs (creation of content, paid advertising, tools, outside consultant, etc.)	See chapter 5
Where am I hosting my content:	– my own website with a blogging platform	See chapter 10
What types of content am I going to be publishing for them (core content):	– blogs – case studies	See chapter 10

(Continued)

Who is going to create that content:	– blogs – me – case studies – me, an outsourced writer and graphic designer	See chapter 10
What type of content created by other people/entities can I share as part of my overall strategy:	– blogs – articles – news	See chapter 7
Regular features or theme for my content:	– Tuesday's Tips (blog every Tuesday) – Thursday's Thoughts (blog every Thursday)	See chapter 10
What do I need to get started creating content:	– what I have: computers, app to record audio – need a graphic artist for design layout for case studies – need a writer/editor for case studies	See chapter 7
Where are the top places my target clients are online (Social media channels):	– LinkedIn – Facebook	See chapter 6
Tools to help with content management and social media marketing	need social moderation tool for scheduling content distribution, comments, mentions and to respond – need cloud based documents, like Google Docs, for content management if more than one person is working on the strategy	See chapter 10

Notice that I included a theme or regular feature section. Think about having a regularly published feature – for example, creating a blog titled *Tuesday's Tips* or *Thursday's Thoughts*. The beauty of this strategy is that it helps to develop a following of fans who can regularly expect and even look forward to reading your thoughts about issues in your area of expertise.

Next, our lawyer Julie would determine roles and responsibilities for those helping with her content development. In the scenario I've created, I've added a few more people as part of her resources. As for your strategy, these roles and responsibilities can be adapted taking into consideration the people available to you as part of your team.

Example Plan
Content Creators: Tactical Roles and Timing

Stages:	Roles & Responsibilities
Content creation	Lawyer: writes blogs, determines how many/how often per month, writes outline for case studies, reviews and approves final versions of case studies Freelance writer: writes case studies Freelance graphic artist: designs layout for case studies and supporting graphics
Content Publishing, Sharing and Promotion	Lawyer: establishes schedule of when her own content is shared, which platforms, communication policy, approves the editorial calendar, identifies sources of other people's content that can be curated and shared, monitors mentions and comments Lawyer's assistant: posts blogs on lawyer's website, schedules the postings of content, finds other people's content to share, fills out editorial calendar, helps share other people's content, monitors comments Webmaster: keeps blogging platform updated with software updates. Consultant: works with lawyer on LinkedIn, Facebook and Google advertising
Listening, Engaging, Monitoring	Lawyer: responds and engages on social media. Lawyer's assistant monitors online conversation. Posts basic "thank you's" as part of engagement and alerts lawyer if anything negative or controversial is posted to determine response
Measuring, Evaluating, Tweaking	Lawyer reviews analytics. Confers with consultant to review marketing results and to tweak strategy as necessary. Lawyer's assistant prepares reports for lawyer to review. Consultant: manages advertising budget, prepares analytics reports for lawyer, and adjusts to meet business objectives

A plan specifying who is responsible at each stage of the content marketing process requires thoughtful consideration in order to make sure that your efforts are paying off. Here's another way of looking at our fictional lawyer, Julie's plan and who is involved.

Tactical Roles and Responsibilities

CREATE CONTENT	MANAGE AND CURATE	ENGAGE AND LISTEN	MEASURE AND ADJUST
Lawyer > Writes blogs, determines how many/how often per month, writes outline for case studies, reviews and approves final versions of case studies.	**Lawyer >** Establishes schedule of when her own content is shared, which platforms, communication policy, approves the editorial calendar, identifies sources of other people's content that can be curated and shared, monitors mentions and comments.	**Lawyer >** Responds and engages on social media.	**Lawyer >** Reviews analytics. Confers with consultant to review marketing results and to tweak strategy as necessary.
Freelance Writer > Writes case studies.	**Lawyer's Assistant >** Posts blogs on lawyers website, schedules the postings of content, finds other people's content to share, fills out editorial calendar, helps share other people's content, monitors comments.	**Lawyer's Assistant >** Monitors online conversation. Posts basic "thank you's" as part of engagement and alerts lawyer if anything negative or controversial is posted to determine response.	**Lawyer's Assistant >** Prepares reports for lawyer to review.
Freelance Graphic Artist > Designs layout for case studies and supporting graphics.	**Webmaster >** Keeps blogging platform updated with software updates.		**Consultant >** Manages advertising budget, prepares analytics reports for lawyer, and adjusts to meet business objectives.
	Consultant > Works with lawyer on LinkedIn, Facebook and Google advertising.		

CONTENT CREATORS

CONTENT MANAGERS

TECHNOLOGY AND ONLINE EXPERTS	SOCIAL MEDIA MONITORS	ANALYTICS CONSULTANT

I delve further into the engaging and listening process in the next chapter.

Now that it's clear who is doing what, the next part of the process comprises three documents or templates. The first is a content planner and tracker. This help organize and track the content you're creating, ensuring it aligns with your business objectives, as well as tracking when and where you are publishing the content. You can use a simple spreadsheet that includes the following information:

Content Planner and Tracking

- Inventory number
- Type of content (blog, video, white paper, case study, etc.)

- Target Audience (client persona profiles that encompass your target audiences or their influencers)
- SEO keywords for the content pieces
- Headline or title for content piece
- Call to Action (what you want people to do)
- Business Objective
- Decision point in the buying cycle
- Content creator (who will write, shoot, design, etc.)
- Content editor (who will proofread, fact check, etc.)
- Due date for content completion
- Where the content is hosted (firm website, syndicating content, etc.)
- Publication date
- Marketing channels (Where are you promoting online and even offline if appropriate)

Content Calendaring

Next is your publishing schedule and for this, you'll be using a document called a content calendar. Publishing your own content and posting on social media, whether once a week, twice a week, monthly, or daily, is dependent on your time and resources.

I recommend a monthly calendar template to track what content you are posting, where you are posting it, and how often.

Here's an example of how this system would work. Establish how often you're going to publish a blog. Using our environmental lawyer, Julie, as an example, let's say her schedule is twice a week, on Mondays and Thursdays. She's using her personal LinkedIn profile and her personal Twitter account to promote. Note that a lawyer could also have a LinkedIn Company Page, as well as a Twitter account for the firm. But to keep it simple for this example, I've only taken into account personal profiles and use "LI" to mean LinkedIn and "TW" to mean Twitter. Once a month, she plans to release a case study, on the first Tuesday of every month and promote it again on the third Wednesday of every month. On the other posting days of the month, she plans to share other people's content (OPC), which she likely will find at least several times a week, if not daily, and plug into the content calendar.

In the example that follows, I've only filled out OPC for the first week, but you'll quickly get the idea. You'll want to look for fresh content every week so those sections will be updated weekly. Additionally, our environmental lawyer is participating in a panel presentation for business owners, and promotion of that event is added to the calendar, as well.

A monthly content calendar in this scenario would look something like the following:

in   CONTENT CALENDAR   🐦

SUNDAY	MONDAY	TUESDAY	WEDNESDAY	THURSDAY	FRIDAY	SATURDAY
	LI - Blog: Changes in Environmental Laws in California TW - Blog: Changes in Environmental Laws in California LI: Promote Panel Presentation TW: Promote Panel Presentation	LI - Case Study TW - Case Study	LI - Article from WSJ about California's environmental challenges TW - Article from WSJ about California's environmental challenges	LI - Blog: Top 3 Questions TW - Blog: Top 3 Questions	LI - Blog from environmental expert on California's clean water act TW - Blog from environmental expert on California's clean water act	LI: Promote Panel Presentation TW: Promote Panel Presentation
LI - Environmental Pollution Infographic - source: Environmental Magazine TW - Environmental Pollution Infographic - source: Environmental Magazine	LI - Blog: Recap of panel presentation TW - Blog: Recap of panel presentation			LI - Blog: What you need to know about reducing toxic air pollutants TW - Blog: What you need to know about reducing toxic air pollutants		
	LI - Blog: New EPA Proposed Ozone Standards Will Have Significant Impacts on California Industry TW - Blog: New EPA Proposed Ozone Standards Will Have Significant Impacts on California Industry		LI - Case Study TW - Case Study	LI - Blog: Top environmental law problems for business owners TW - Blog: Top environmental law problems for business owners		

Editorial Calendar

The third template or document is an editorial calendar showing the exact words, photos, images, etc., of all postings. This is the daily plan that ties together the content, marketing channels, dates, and what you're posting to achieve your objectives. The following shows the information I recommend you track on this calendar, which also can easily be done with an Excel spreadsheet. Again, I've used the environmental lawyer as an example, including her target audiences and business objectives.

- Week - start date (most current week on top)
- Scheduled date to be posted
- Time of day (include time zone)

	A	B	C	D	E	F	G	H	I	J	K	L	M	N	O
	Week - Start Date (most current week on top)	Scheduled Date to be Posted/ Tweeted	Time of Day (Include Time Zone)	Approval: Person Initials and Date	LinkedIn	Twitter MESSAGING (140 CHARACTERS)	Event Related Tweets	Event Related Posts for LinkedIn	Target Audience	Description of Content (Image, video, etc.) if applicable AND source of content	Link to image in Photo Folder on Google Docs or videos	Description of External Links (i.e. Shell's link driving to landing page, NCLR registration page, YouTube video, etc.)	Business Objective or Purpose	Hashtag	Confirmed that it posted
1															
2															
3															

- Approval - person's initials and date
  (This is relevant if you have someone else writing your social media posts and then the posts need your approval prior to posting)
- Platforms:
  - LinkedIn
  - Twitter
- Event related Tweets
- Event related posts for LinkedIn
- Target audience
- Description of content (blog, image, video, etc. if applicable AND source of content if other people's content)
- Link to image in photo folder on Google Docs or videos (this is where you're hosting photos you're using in your posts, or where you're hosting videos)
- Description of external links -(where is the link driving to)
- Business objective or purpose for each posting
- Hashtag(s)
- Confirmation once posted and date

Up until now, the strategy and process has been comprised of a lot of thinking and planning. Now we can move on to implementing tools to help support your strategy and the actual creation work, and save time.

Software Tools and Resources for Content Marketing

Many free and inexpensive online tools are available to help with managing your content and social media strategy, and new tools are emerging all the time. Below are some options that are currently on the market and well liked that can help save time:

To manage content and publication of that content you can use tools such as:

- Hootsuite
- Tweetdeck
- Buffer
- Sprout Social

The software tools above allow you to schedule your posts across various social media channels all at once, saving you time and allowing the posts to be published on whatever date and time you choose. These can be invaluable, given your busy schedule and the potentially limited time you may have to dedicate to social media marketing. The tools also let you search for other people's content using hashtags, as described earlier. Most also provide analytics, such as reach of message, audience size, and new followers on your account. They additionally allow for multiple people to manage a social media account with a pro account, which is helpful if you have others working on this with you.

The tools and resources for content creation below help you create pieces of content such as images with words, infographics, catchy headlines, blogs, and email newsletters. Using tools like these can help create some of your simple content in a cost-efficient manner – and most are pretty straightforward to use.

- Headline Analyzer
- Canva
- PicMonkey
- iStock
- Constant Contact
- Mail Chimp
- Piktochart
- Visual.ly
- Contently
- YouZign

New tools and software surface often so I recommend you search online for best tools and software using keywords such as

- "best social media tools"
- "best email marketing software"
- "top content marketing tools"
- "best social media monitoring"

Also try variations of those for reviews and recommendations.

Paid Advertising

There is one other significant way to promote your content, as well as your social media profiles, that we have yet to discuss, and that is using paid advertising on social media platforms. Some platforms offer the ability to pay for sponsored posts or tweets. Therefore, their algorithms are created in a way that only a small portion of your followers will see your posts at any given time – unless you advertise, which then exposes your content to more people.

Other platforms don't offer advertising – yet. If you have a marketing budget, implementing paid advertising can help boost your efforts when you don't have a large following. Each platform is different, however, and you can spend a lot of money quickly without seeing significant results if you're not comfortable with how to implement targeting and demographic strategies. I would recommend consulting with a social media marketing expert who can explain, teach, and even implement and manage a paid advertising campaign on your behalf. It is cost efficient to hire someone who knows what they're doing versus trying it yourself and wasting money by not knowing how to optimize your advertising campaigns.

11 Engaging, Listening, and Responding

All of the processes and steps outlined up to this point have been about alignment – alignment between strategy, tactics, and goals. This alignment is critical to ensuring you see meaningful results. However, publishing and marketing your content is only part of an effective strategy.

The other part is engaging with and listening to your fans and followers. Your blogs, videos, case studies, webinars etc., now become the beginning of a conversation. Engagement means actions that involve you in a public dialogue, such as tweeting back a response to people who have questions, acknowledging compliments or positive feedback about your content, or, very importantly, addressing concerns or complaints, which we'll discuss later in this chapter.

The key in this process is that you're building relationships by engaging with your target audiences. You might ask questions of your audience on social media to start conversations, follow people back on Twitter or re-tweet their tweets, and through doing so help build a relationship with that user. Calls to action, such as "Like if you agree" or "Tag someone who would like this post," are also conversation starters and audience growers, encouraging your fan base to share your message and branding.

Listening to online conversations that directly involve you seems like common sense, but it's also beneficial to listen to conversations happening around your area of specialty, your competition, your clients, and your industry.

Here's why:

- Participating in social discussions around your areas of expertise helps establish your credibility.
- You can identify opportunities to create content addressing a topic you hadn't considered.

- Stumbling upon conversations about your personal brand or industry can help you with reputation management.
- Questions and answers found by listening can help create a knowledge base.
- It's possible you would uncover conversations about intent to find an expert ("Can anyone recommend...?" or "I need ...").
- Keeping an ear out for discontent with competitors might give you ideas on messages to incorporate into your marketing.
- Staying "in the know" about your clients can lead to ideas on how to be of further value to them or with client retention strategies.
- Potentially what you find may help with recruiting, as well as identifying experts and influencers.

What to Monitor

Here are a few ideas on what to monitor:

- Your name, common misspellings of your name, and your firm name
- Keywords (and hashtags, such as #environmental) that are relevant to you, your firm, your area of specialty, and even key legal matters in your state
- Your clients' names, their industries, and legal issues related to them
- Sentiment around your name and firm name
- Names of your competitors

In the last section of this chapter, I go over tools available to you to help "listen" online. The other critical reason to be listening to social media channels and other content channels, such as YouTube and Yelp, is for reputation management and crisis communications. With social media, you should operate as if the potential for someone to "broadcast" their discontent about you is likely. It's not a matter of if, it's a matter of when. So being in the conversation right away can help to diffuse any difficult situations and save your online reputation.

For these and other reasons, establishing a process for listening and responding is in your best interest. Think about the following as you develop your plan for this critical element:

- Who will be regularly listening
- What messages will prompt responses or notifications:
  - Someone says something bad or good about you, your firm, or a post
  - Someone asks a question
  - Someone is talking about a need for your services
  - The sentiment in a conversation stream is getting very negative
  - Hostile postings or threats
- For notifications, figure out who's notified for their input and how (text, call, email, etc.)
- Who is authorized to respond on your behalf, and does the response need to be vetted or does that person have authority to respond (more on that in the next chapter about creating your social media policy)
- Including Twitter direct messages, LinkedIn InMail, and Facebook messages in your listening process as some will elect to communicate with you privately

These issues need to be thought out and carefully planned because, as mentioned, a communication misstep can quickly damage your reputation.

As a general rule, responses should be posted in the channels that the original comments, complaints, or hostile postings appeared. Keep in mind that responding is about being transparent and helpful. Ultimately, the goal should be strengthening relationships. Avoid legalese whenever possible. Responses should be crafted in a conversational tone as if you were face to face with the other person.

Dealing with Complaints and Negative Comments on Social Media

I'm often asked whether every negative comment or complaint requires a response. More often than not, the answer to this is yes. Rather than shy away from complaints, use them as opportunities to demonstrate you care about the other person. Publicly acknowledging a criticism, in a manner such as, "Sorry to hear you had that experience. Please send me a direct message with your contact information so we can learn more and work to resolve the issue," first, helps to diffuse someone's anger; second, it moves the discussion offline; and finally, it shows the world you care and that you're not ignoring people. The public is often less interested in the complainer's issue and more interested in how you respond. Acting swiftly and with empathy can actually help your reputation.

On occasion, you may have what is called "flaming," hostile, insulting, profanity-laced comments. Often, you can't reason with these individuals. Their comments portray them negatively, and most people will see it for what it is. Your choices are (1) to let it go and not respond; (2) to report them to the platform as allowed on some social channels; (3) to delete the comment; (4) ban them from posting as allowed for on some social channels; (5) or hide their comment.

For example on Facebook, you're able to hide a comment so it's not visible to others but still visible to the person who wrote the comment. It all depends on how you feel about the situation. Sometimes not responding is the right strategy because then you don't inflame the situation further and add to the "drama." If a negative comment has a question included, you need to decide whether or not to address the question. Take into consideration whether the answer would have value to others.

Timing of your responses is important, as well. Address complaints quickly —within 6-12 hours, and even faster if it's an issue that can quickly spiral into a reputational issue. Here's the key - internal planning ties to external reputation management for you and your firm. This planning can be documented in a social media policy that guides your colleagues and employees with regard to social media, or it can be a separate document to guide whomever is helping you with your social media marketing. I go further into what a social media policy should cover in the next chapter. But first, let's review some tools to help your listening and engagement.

Some tools that we've already described for use with content management, such as Hootsuite and TweetDeck, are also useful for listening and responding. Subscribing to sentiment software is also an option. Various third-party solutions can be found with a simple online search.

There is also the free must-have: Google Alerts. You can set up these alerts to be sent to you regularly when keywords, names, or phrases are mentioned on the Internet. If you do nothing else, at least set these free alerts up so you are aware of any mentions of you and your brand online. Note that they only monitor what is findable on search engines, and not anything posted in closed platforms like Facebook and LinkedIn, but this would be better than no monitoring at all and is a start, at a minimum.

12 Social Media Policy

A social media policy is much like an employee manual that guides employees who post content on the Internet as part of their responsibilities. The purpose of having one is to set expectations of appropriate behavior, to prevent exposing the company to legal problems or public embarrassment, and to provide guidance on what to do when a negative or tricky situation comes up and it's not clear in the policy what to do. The bottom line – it's protection for you and your employees.

Several notorious social media disasters that have scared lawyers away from embracing social media marketing might have been avoided if there was a social media policy in place educating their employees about proper behavior and the risks of not using good judgment.

So when should you put a policy in place? The minute you go from one person to two or more people executing your strategy and creating content for you or communicating on your behalf online. If you're not yet active on social media but you have more than two employees, you need to have one in place as well, because the employees are also an extension of your brand. Think about all the places through which they can be "tied" to your firm: by adding where they work on their LinkedIn profile, in their work and education section on their Facebook profile, tagged in a photo with a colleague in the office, etc.

So where do you begin in writing this policy and what should be included? I often tell lawyers when drafting a policy that they need to think about not just the elements of the policy itself, but the tone and tenor of how it's worded and what it communicates to your team.

By the sheer nature of being in the legal industry many law firms and management teams tend to be very cautious and conservative about the use of social media. Attorneys, who are always thinking of the worst-case scenarios, often want to create overly restrictive policies. This is counterproductive to your overall business objectives.

Consider that your employees can actually help you raise awareness about your brand, as well as help create goodwill for you and your practice. If their postings show they are happy at work, or they exhibit pride by being associated with you and your firm, that can help in your recruitment process. This is also another data point for potential clients to develop a favorable impression about you. If your staff shares your content, they are using their sphere of influence, and that can be beneficial to your client attraction goals.

When creating a policy, I recommend you think of your staff as advocates and not potential adversaries and create a policy is really establishing parameters and not trying to control everything they do online.

I've seen policies that are 15 pages long, and I've seen others that are as simple as a few words. According to Tony Hsieh, CEO of Zappo's, the company's Twitter policy is: Just be real. And use your best judgment.

As attorneys, you probably want a bit more, since you have ethical considerations, especially around client confidentiality. But the prevailing approach should be short and sweet, as well as positive. Focus on a general policy, rather than pages and pages of excruciating detail about every platform. A long and overly cautious policy can be a disincentive and can stall a good social media strategy in its tracks. If this recommendation makes you uncomfortable, and you're thinking about all the publicized stories you've heard about lawyers and social media, refer back to chapter 3 which talks about legal risks.

A policy should be customized for you and your practice. Depending on the size of your firm, you may want to get input from your firm's most important stakeholders, including your managers, IT experts, marketers and even the Gen Y or millennials. We've included the firm's marketers in this list because your law firm's brand is important.

Here are the typical elements that are addressed in a social media policy:

Interactions, Communications, and General Behavior. These include the proper way to engage with others online, acceptable and not acceptable behavior, your firm's tone of communication, i.e., friendly but professional, respectful, never condescending, not hostile, etc. Be sure your employees are keenly aware that anyone can and will potentially read their social postings, including current clients, potential future clients, peers, and even future employers. Any insensitive or inappropriate posts can alienate one of these sets of people and damage both the employee and the firm in some way. Using good judgment is of paramount importance in this area, as the firm could be reflected upon badly if comments by an employee are seen in a negative light.

Confidential, Proprietary, and Copyrighted Information. Clearly outline what types of information should not be shared about the firm and its clients. This should include not only words used in postings, but photos, as well. Any use of copyrighted information should, of course, be given credit and attribution as is necessary under the law.

Postings and representing the firm. Information that the staff posts online should not be attributed to the firm or appear to be endorsed by the firm unless the content being shared is something like a firm blog, etc. If they are unsure, they should avoid posting and/or ask an appropriate person. If they are able to use the firm's name, what is the proper way to refer to the firm, and other pertinent branding guidance?

Internal matters. Provide guidance on how to handle unhappiness and dissatisfaction in regard to something occurring at the firm and not posting about the situation online.

Avoid giving advice. Consider information on your state bar's ethics rules about what could be considered giving advice in this scenario, as well as how best to respond to people who are asking questions on your social platforms. For example, you might provide an example of how to respond online, such as, "I'm sorry, we can't answer that question directly. To give you the best answer, we would need more information about your particular circumstance. You could make an appointment to come in, so we can learn more and make sure we provide you the right information."

Be truthful. Address the need for accuracy in their online biographies, comments, and postings, along with avoidance of information that could be perceived as misleading. This includes use of the words "expert" or "specialized," unless it's defensible, as well as the encouragement to acknowledge and correct any errors quickly. Also, guidance to be transparent and recommendations about not posting or commenting anywhere anonymously should be included.

Online recommendations for colleagues or testimonials. Your firm's stance about posting recommendations online. If done, is it their own personal recommendation or the firm's recommendation? Suggest who to clear these types of postings with in advance of posting.

Stay on the right side of the law. A reminder to avoid any on-line activity or posting of information that violates laws or ethics rules or could be perceived as possible violations.

Who is responsible. Inform your team who they should go to for a decision if they're not clear on what to do about something not covered in the social media policy.

Privacy. Your firm's view on the privacy of the employee's individual profiles. Should they expect that the firm may be monitoring what they post on their own Facebook, Instagram, and other profiles?

Consequences. State clearly what will happen if policies are violated and preventive actions they can take to avoid violations. As in, if in doubt, don't move ahead – ask first.

Good judgment. Consider ending with the most paramount mes-sage. You encourage the use of social media, and the most important thing to remember is to use good judgment. Just like in the offline world, the online world is no different in your request that your staff use good judgment.

You may very likely have others supporting you in your social media marketing. For example, you may decide to have someone post on your behalf, monitor online conversations, or even help with creation of your content. You will have processes in place (or should), as covered in the strategy section of this book, about communicating to the outside world. You will also have particulars about the content you're creating and pub-lishing, covered in the content creation and strategy sections of this book. If so, these are additional areas that should be referenced in your policy. For example, what are the procedures that should be followed, and where are those procedures are documented?

If at all possible, be sure to educate the staff on the policy, rather than simply having them read it. Spend time training and giving examples of both good and bad activities, proper engagement with others online, and training the staff on the ins and outs of the policy so they can be set up for success. Also, consider bringing someone in periodically to update your team on the newest trends in social media platforms as part of your train-ing plan. New issues will surface with each platform. This approach can go a long way in communicating your encouragement about the use of social media and creating a positive social culture. Through it, you will empower them with useful and helpful information, and you will have enthusiastic employees who can become evangelists for your firm.

It's important to review your social media policy frequently, as social media platforms change often and trends shift quickly. At the very minimum, the policy should be reviewed once a year.

If writing one from scratch seems daunting, you can find online many examples of social media policies from Fortune 500 companies to smaller companies to refer to when drafting your own.

13 What Measurements Equate to Success

In order for social media and content marketing to help you achieve your business objectives, you need to measure outcomes and actions. The analytics I'm talking about here are not just number of fans or "likes." Having a large number of followers is less relevant than having a smaller number of the right types of fans who are actively engaged, interested, and calling your office. If your business objective is to bring in three more big clients over the course of the year, you may only need 1,000 quality followers who are taking the desired actions to achieve your business objectives. In fact, until your social media fans have helped you meet your goals, the value of the total number of them is zero.

Measuring your social media efforts also includes the ability to determine if you're publishing content that your target audience likes. You need to assess pretty quickly if the platforms you're using are yielding the best results, so if they are not, you can change your strategy or spend your efforts on the platforms that are providing the best ROI instead. Part of the assessment of your strategy should also include measuring sentiment, or positive mentions versus negative mentions. Too much of a negative sentiment can cause a potential client to choose another attorney.

As you well know, time is money, especially in the legal industry. Ultimately, your goal is to generate more revenue. This chapter will give you insights into what and how to measure, and what to do with that information. My goal is for you to spend as little time as necessary with the greatest impact possible.

What to Measure

In order to know what to measure, you need to go back and start with why you're making these efforts in the first place. Earlier in this book, I covered getting clear on why you're implementing a social strategy

and identifying your business goals and objectives with measurable outcomes. You may want to refer to the business objectives template you
filled out.

> To access the Business Objectives Template go to
> www.MicheleRuiz.com/ContentMarketingResources.

For example, let's say you're an adoption lawyer in the Great Lakes
region. One objective might be to bring in six more clients from your area
within the next 12 months who want to adopt a child. Remember, they
should be "SMART" or specific, measurable, attainable, realistic, and timely
(within a time frame).

The ultimate success barometer is the effectiveness of your content
and its ability to drive potential clients to contact you. But the steps
you are using to get that result are also important to evaluate. Using the
adoption scenario, you have decided to write blog posts that provide information about adoption-related matters. You host those blogs on your
website and distribute them on Facebook, as well, because you know
women are key decision makers in adoption matters and the predominant
users on this platform. You are also implementing a newsletter strategy to
promote your blog and have a sign-up form on your website.

So what should you measure in this scenario?

- Traffic to your website – is it growing?
- Website visitors - are the visitors coming from your desired geo-
  graphic area in the country? In this example, it would be predomi-
  nantly in the Great Lakes region.
- Website traffic referrers – is the increased traffic coming from
  Facebook or Google search engines? Or in some other way, such as
  someone mentioned your blog online and that mention is driving a
  lot of traffic to your website?
- Time spent on your website - are your website visitors spending
  time on your website? If so, it's an indicator they're finding information they want or is valuable to them.
- Top landing pages - which pages on your website are getting the
  most traffic? Are they mostly landing on your blog page or your
  About Us page? The key is to understand if they are landing and
  spending time on the page(s) that help your business objectives.

- Contact us form - are requests for an appointment via the online form going up?
- Newsletter sign up form — are there growing numbers of people signing up for your newsletter? What pages are leading to the most sign-ups? Is it a specific blog or the newsletter sign up button on your home page?
- Target demographic - are the new sign-ups mostly the desired potential clients or referrers you want?
- Newsletter open rates — do you have good open rate percentages of your newsletter? Are they going up and not down?
- Newsletter click through rates — once opened, are they clicking through and landing on your website on the desired page(s)?
- Newsletter shares — are people sharing your newsletter with others, indicating that they are finding the information valuable? Are those share numbers going up?
- Blog posts on your website — Are they getting traffic? Is it the right kind of traffic? Is the number of followers of your blog growing?
- Blog comments - are they actively engaged by commenting and sharing? Is the number of comments going up the longer you have been blogging?
- The demographics of Facebook followers — their age, gender, and location where they live. Are the majority within your desired demographic?
- Facebook posts — are people liking, sharing, and commenting on your blog-related posts? Are the numbers of people who are engaging going up?
- Sentiment of comments — are the comments positive or complimentary about the information you're sharing? What is the percentage of positive versus negative? What does the trend look like?
- Questions via social — are people asking you questions? Are those types of comments going up?
- Click-throughs back to your website from Facebook — is the trend going up over time?
- Total reach — the number of people who were served any activity from your page, including your posts, posts to your page by other people, page likes, ads, mentions, and check-ins. In other words, the total number of people who could have seen your content by any number of actions. Are those numbers going up?

- Client inquiries from social media - how many new client leads came from social media or content you shared? Is it a decent enough percentage for your business objectives? How many referrals came from blogs you shared on social media?
- Influence metrics – are you considered an online influencer based on your influence metrics? Are those numbers going up or down? Are the topics you're considered an influencer in relevant to your business goals?
- Your evangelists - who is actively sharing and commenting positively on your content? It's important to keep building a relationship with them.
- Expertise requests – has anyone reached out to you to ask you to speak, contribute to a presentation, provide an interview, quoted your blog, or more based on seeing you or your content online?
- New clients – finally, has the number of new clients as you defined in your business objective gone up?

The content marketing and social media strategy for the adoption lawyer in this fictional scenario is basic. It's one type of content, one social media platform, plus email marketing and a website. Now, let's assume you, as the adoption lawyer, have been implementing the strategy for four months. In that time period, you've:

- Published eight blogs on the blogging platform on your website
- Posted about those blogs on your business-related Facebook page and have shared other content related to adoption matters
- Pushed out your blog using your email newsletter eight times

Here's how data points can help finesse the strategy. The metrics show two of the blog posts related to rights of biological mothers and fathers had higher numbers of comments, and the highest amount of Facebook likes and shares in comparison to the blog posts created about documentation for international adoption. The analytics for the newsletter showed that the topics related to rights were clicked on the most, even though there were various items covered in the newsletters. Website traffic numbers showed people were landing on the About Us page on your website. Only three percent of those users went from that page to the Contact

Us page and only two people filled out the online lead form to get more information. Both of those people were not from the Great Lakes region.

Let's assume that the sign-ups for your newsletter went up 15% in that initial time period. The following on your Facebook page went from 146 fans to 583 in that four-month period. The data points also show that when you used Facebook to share an article from the newspaper about adoptive parents battling the biological father and whether or not he had rights to rescind the adoption, that particular posting generated a noticeable engagement and lively discussion from fans. One of the commenters asked a question about the process to adopt. You went ahead and created a blog about the top ten most important things to know about the process of adoption, shared it, and responded to that commenter to read the blog post you wrote about that topic.

In this hypothetical scenario, we know that biological rights are generating significantly more interest and engagement than the other topics you wrote about. We also know from the analytics that a certain percentage of people are taking the desired action, which is to click through to your site, and hopefully filling out the Contact Us form. But the analytics also show the conversion rate isn't that great. People are landing on the About Us page and leaving the website, without you gathering the contact information needed to be able to reach out to them.

Using the data, you tweak certain aspects of your strategy. You write more blogs about the topic of biological rights and use the case mentioned in the article that got a lot of engagement about the rights of biological fathers as the basis for several additional blogs. You mention in the blogs that you practice in the Great Lakes region. You change the links from your newsletter to go to the main page on your website, where your blogs are featured and a Call to Action (CTA) is prominently displayed to fill out the Contact Us online form.

In month five and six, the numbers continue to go up related to Facebook fans and newsletter sign-ups. But now the website traffic analytics show people are landing on the home page, spending more time on your website blog pages, and the conversion rates – how many people have filled out the Contact Us form – have increased by 19%. And four people who filled out the Contact Us page were from the desired geographical regions. Two of those made appointments, leading to your goal of six more clients in one year.

Remember that blog post created about the top ten things to know about the process of adoption as a response to one commenter? A reporter found that post, and called you for a quote to include in a media article. You just earned media coverage. You didn't pay for it like one would pay for advertising, and it helped your branding as an expert in adoption matters.

Again, this is a hypothetical scenario, but I've seen similar outcomes over and over with the clients my company works with across all industries. Using data and "listening" to the online community via their comments and tweaking the strategy in some simple ways can lead a higher ROI and ultimately more of the right kind of potential clients reaching out.

If you go back and look at all the data points that can and should be measured for a scenario like this, it can seem overwhelming. Here's what you need to keep in mind: once you've set up your tools and use a simple form to look at the data in one place, you're really paying attention to trends and what is really working. Once you get accustomed to how to look at the data, it'll take you less and less time; and in just a few minutes, you'll be able to see trends and where you should spend time tweaking your strategy for better, more optimal results.

Now that I've provided you an example, let's talk about you and your strategy. As I've mentioned, it is important to know up front what "success" means to you and your efforts and understand the measurable outcomes you are aiming for.

Those objectives and outcomes can vary widely. Is success, for example, attracting five more commercial real estate clients who own strip centers in the Denver area over the next nine months? Or is success hosting six webinars over the next 12 months on the topics of mergers and acquisitions and, from them, having 20 potential corporate clients participate and contact you? Perhaps it's a goal of 1,000 potential clients who have signed up to get your blog delivered to their email address, or 500 downloads of your eBook on setting up a living trust from potential clients in the Los Angeles area. Whatever the case may be, it's important to set the objective in order to attempt to achieve it.

Also, what do you want your target audience to do? Is it that they fill out a lead form, or share your video with their own social media network? Is it that they retweet your latest shared link? Knowing up front what actions you'd like them to take helps you to understand at the end of the day if your strategies and content are serving your purposes.

Managing What You're Measuring

You may be asking, "How do I know what 'good' performance is?" To answer that, you need to review six groups of data: (1) your website traffic and user activity data; (2) social media metrics; (3) content related numbers; (4) sentiment information; (5) PR and thought leadership results; and (6) paid advertising analytics.

Website Traffic and User Activity

Website data is critical, in particular to help drive conversion. This is where, more often than not, referrers or potential clients will be influenced to contact you. It's also critical for those people to get an impression about your practice, and, if it's favorable, their visit to your site can likely lead to more people reaching out to you. As mentioned in the strategy section of this book, your website is an important component.

Basically, you'll be evaluating which elements are the true traffic drivers to your website, such as one social media platform over another, links from your email newsletter, or search engine results. You'll also want to glean if visitors are landing on the page you want them to and if it's leading to conversions. If you host downloadable content on your site, how is that content performing? If you're getting a lot of good traffic from your content, but not enough conversions, it may be related to the messaging and construct of your site.

Conversely, if you're not getting any significant traffic from your content or your social platforms, that's indicative that the content and social media platforms need to be re-evaluated. Is it the topics you're choosing? Maybe you've forgotten to include calls to actions in your content, such as "find out more now" or "visit our site to," in order to help increase the likelihood that the user will click over to your website. Is the social platform the right one? If it is, are you maximizing the strategies for that platform? You might want to refer to the strategy chapter of this book for more information on these and other similar questions about performance.

If you're using content such as blogs to promote in-person educational events, and you're capturing those RSVPs on your website, you will also want to track where the RSVP leads are coming from online, how many people RSVP'd, and of those, how many actually attended.

With the use of tools like Google Analytics, Moz Analytics, Clicky, and KISSMetrics, you can learn a lot about all things related to your website. I suggest starting with Google Analytics, which is by far the most popular and free. If there's more data that you want to capture that Google Analytics doesn't offer, such as individual user actions, there are solutions that are available by subscription.

If this seems overwhelming or not something you want to spend your time pulling together, I highly recommend using a consultant to set up the metrics, process and reports for you. They might even be the ones who then provide you recommendations to improve your results. It's a necessary step and worth the investment.

Direct Social Metrics and Content Data

In the context of using content marketing and social media for growing your book of business, you would be capturing data that is important for your lead generation strategy. Ultimately, you want to look at analytics that tie to referrers of clients and potential clients. The more users who choose to 'follow" you or your business profiles, the higher your ability to find potential clients. These types of metrics typically include:

- Fan / follower count and growth trends
- Demographics, including gender, age, and location
- Engagement on platform(s)
- Which platform(s) are driving the most traffic to your website
- Social sentiment around you and your brand
- Social stats on your competitors

Metrics such as likes, "shares," and "views" all relate to the actions the target audience is doing once they see your content on social media platforms. Much like driving website traffic, you want to motivate the user to either share your content on their network, like it so their network sees it, or comment on it in order to engage with you or your firm. In addition, you want to extend your reach and following. The more people who share your content, the larger your reach (the overall total of users in the networks of those who share your content) becomes. You will be analyzing numbers that speak to the following:

- What types of posts are popular with your audience?
- Is your informational content, such as blogs, eBooks, and webinars, getting you more exposure and leads?
- The overall "reach" of your content
- Are people taking the actions and steps online that lead them to hire you as their lawyer, and are those numbers growing?

This kind of measuring helps you answer the question, "How do I get more leads through my efforts?" First, you'll want to become familiar with the dashboards of the social media platforms you're using, such as LinkedIn Twitter, and Facebook. On LinkedIn, you can see who's viewed your profile and who is engaging with what you post and content you share. On your LinkedIn company page, if you have one for your firm, you'll want to assess how many likes and comments you're receiving, and engagement data for your posts, including content you create and other people's content you share. You can also identify demographic information of those following your firm page, such as industry, seniority level within a company, their job function, and more.

Then you want to get familiar with some specific marketing data. For example, with an account on Twitter, you can get a demographic portrait of your followers by age, gender, education level, income, interests, location, and more, and assess how your posted content is performing, as well as how your profile is performing overall.[37] Facebook also has a dashboard with similar types of data.

Besides the integrated dashboards, numerous tools exist that help. Some are all encompassing, allowing you to manage your strategy and postings, and they provide analytics, as well. Tools such as Hootsuite, Sprout Social, and Cyfe are some in this category, and pricing options vary.

Sentiment

It's difficult to get the most out of your investment if you're not monitoring what is being said about you and how people feel about you and your brand. Another very important area of measurement is users' sentiment, or the "feeling" and tone of posts and interactions. Although software tools exist to tabulate total mentions of keywords like your name and brand, a person, rather than software, will need to review and decide on the interactions and whether they have more of a positive or a negative bent to them.

Staying on top of sentiment can help guide your content strategy. If it's negative, you should consider what you can do to change the tone of the online conversation. If it's positive, keep doing what you're doing. If it's neutral, you need to focus on more ways to get people to talk about you online and via social media. Once you know how your target audience is viewing your content, and more broadly, you or your firm as a whole, you can make adjustments and optimizations to improve the sentiment if need be.

To start, set up a Google Alerts for every term associated with you, your firm, and your brand. Also consider setting up Google Alerts for your competitors and industry. Monitoring sentiment around these can give you ideas for your strategy and content to share. Don't forget to set up alerts for your clients and their industries, too. Information may surface that gives you a reason to contact your client or publish a white paper that speaks to a timely issue related to a big client, providing you with an opportunity to show that you can be of additional value. While free and a good place to start, Google Alerts is known to miss mentions on Twitter and Facebook. There are also solutions such as Hootsuite, Social Mention, and others to monitor online conversations.

Public Relations and Thought Leadership Metrics

If you are implementing a PR strategy, even if it's an SEO PR strategy as covered in chapter 9, you definitely want to be looking at some data to see what kind of impact you're making. Even if you're not focused on those strategies, just doing content marketing can land you the attention of journalists and influential bloggers, so there's no downside in tracking some numbers. We're not talking about generating buzz as many PR people promote. In today's world of social media and marketing, no one has the resources to simply generate buzz, and it's too vague to measure. Remember, to support your business goals efficiently and effectively, everything you're doing has to have some metrics to measure.

If you've issued press releases through a wire service, there are metrics available such as placements, pickups, circulation, total reach, and impressions. But these are not enough, because there are a lot of sites that automatically publish press releases as new pages on their sites in order to increase their content to enable them to accept and post more advertising. What really matters is if there are any mentions of your blog, and if anyone is calling you for an interview. Is anyone of influence sharing your information and validating that you're a thought leader? Do you have brand evangelists, who are enthusiastic and loyal fans of what you're publishing, and who frequently engage and share your content?

Besides tracking bloggers' mentions of your content and how often it's happening, it's also important to track the people who really like what you post so you can engage with them further. Also, knowing the number of journalists who are following you can be key to garnering further subject matter expert engagements. Have you had any requests for interviews, or have you been quoted in any media? There are also tools to help identify who is influential online, such as Klout, PeerIndex and Kred. The key here is looking at the trend and whether or not your influencer numbers are going up.

Social Media Advertising

If you've decided to incorporate social media advertising to boost your reach quickly, there will be additional analytics to review. If you've taken my recommendation to bring in a consultant to help you initially with the paid campaigns in order to be the most effective with your spending, then there will be reporting that will give you analytics. These will include cost-per-click, cost-per-impression, cost-per-engagement, reach and total spent and even more. In the end, you're measuring the cost-per-lead and optimizing to continue ensuring you're spending the lowest amount possible for the strongest results.

As technology is always changing, new tools to collect the metrics are constantly being created. The latest list of tools I recommend, called "Measuring Social Media ROI," is available on my website.

> To access Measuring Social Media ROI document
> www.MicheleRuiz.com/ContentMarketingResources.

In order to get a picture of how your overall strategy is working, you need to aggregate all your data and create your own customized dashboard. There is no need to get fancy, and you don't need a Ph.D. It's basically an Excel spreadsheet customized for the metrics you're tracking.

Once you've collected what you're measuring and are using an Excel spreadsheet, you'll see trends that will become obvious. Ultimately, the purpose of measuring is to know the ROI is worthwhile and the strategy is worth pursuing. Once you see what does and does not work, it is essential that you continually use that data to optimize your content development and distribution strategy.

14 Biggest Mistakes Attorneys Make and How to Avoid Them

It's important to know what to do, and also what not to do when engaging in social media marketing. I've shown you the proper path to the best results. I see many lawyers who make some common mistakes. My goal is for you to generate revenue while spending the least amount of time and having the greatest amount of impact. The following are the top mistakes that can stop your social media effort dead in its tracks, before you ever get it off the ground.

1. Taking on too much

While it might be tempting to go hog wild and join every possible social media platform, the truth is lawyers don't need to be on all of them. It is important to discern those that are the best fit for your objectives and where in the social sphere you will most likely find your potential clients.

You're on social platforms in order to build trust, and relationships on these platforms take time. Spreading yourself too thin by engaging on too many platforms will mean you don't have enough time or resources to implement your strategy well. Concentrate your efforts on the top platforms that you can manage well and are right for your business objectives. For some, it may be just one platform to start. For others, it may be two or three.

The idea of doing too much too early also applies to content. Pick one or two types of content to start your strategy, and get really good at creating that content and implementing the content creation into your workflow before you attempt to create other kinds of content.

2. Me, me and more and me

While building your brand is important, talking too much about yourself, all the accolades you get, and how wonderful your firm is will surely turn off some potential clients. Instead, focus on speaking to the needs your audience might have and what questions they may need answered. The majority of your content should focus on engaging the audience, not selling your services.

Remember to create and share content that has value to the end-user, making it more "shareable" and interesting. Also, be sure to have the right content mix. Consider following the 80/20 rule to guide you when it comes to social media engagement: 80% informational content and 20% promotional posts. On occasion, you can post something personal, like a photo from your morning hike, so people can get to know you as a person, as well.

3. Failing to do your research

While you might be tempted to jump right in, as mentioned above, doing so without understanding who your real audience is and where to find them can lead to a lot of wasted time. Research where your audiences tend to be online and how they use social platforms. Recognize that each social media platform has its own language and way of communicating. Posting the way you do on Twitter with abbreviations within Facebook would be a mistake and can cause people to stop following you.

4. Underestimating the resources needed

One of the biggest mistakes I see clients make is underestimating the depth of the pool they're jumping into. Know your resources and how much of them you are realistically willing to allocate toward your social media strategy, including time. Attorneys often jump in enthusiastically, then get bogged down and post infrequently. Or worse, they give up altogether, and all you hear is crickets on social media. Not being active after starting down this path can convey a negative impression about you, so it is better to not have started than to start and suddenly disappear.

5. Not following a strategy roadmap

Set out from the onset with a "roadmap" of where you're going and how you're going to get there. In other words, create your strategy. Set a schedule, post regularly, and engage your audience. Whatever your target at the end of the road, clearly know it and head toward it as you navigate the social media sphere. A solid plan upfront will be easier to execute on, and you can measure and alter course throughout in order to bring in those clients.

6. Cause a roar, not a snore

Boring content = losing followers. While informative, educational content is bound to be full of facts, arguments, and important points to remember, don't make the mistake of simply putting out your content with no thought about your voice or the mindset of the audience. You may need to lay out the scenario for your audience, much like you might with a jury. Remember, your goal is to offer engaging content. Tell stories. Let your sense of humor, personality, and intellect shine through. Be conversational and avoid legalese, unless you're communicating with other lawyers.

7. Not being ready for the long haul

Starting a social media campaign is not the 50-yard dash, but rather a marathon. It is very common to start out with gusto when beginning a social media effort. But due to impatience, the effort gets derailed and enthusiasm dwindles. It is important to know going in that you need time to build your audience, test different messaging strategies, and measure your results. Expecting your first few posts to "go viral" or get a lot of interaction is simply unrealistic. Can it happen? Of course. Is it guaranteed to happen? Absolutely not. Get to know your potential clients, where they are online, be diligent in your efforts, and your investment will be worthwhile. Have fun with it, and before you know it, you'll find yourself building your client base.

8. Not having consistent branding across your social media platforms

Your brand should be the same on each platform. Use the same photo for your profile pictures on all social media pages, as well as the same description. Try to have the same username, if at all possible. If you're the "Family Law Dude" on one, you should be the "Family Law Dude" everywhere. Consistency is key. You want people to know it's you, no matter where they find you.

9. #DontForgetTheHashtag

Hashtags (#) tied to keywords are extremely useful on social media when it comes to extending your reach and engagement. The simple act of including a hashtag in your post will allow users to see your link, post, or comment when searching for content including that keyword. Hashtags also allow you to reach people who aren't following you. There are also themes such as #ThrowBackThursday or #MotivationMonday that you can join in on. And one other #tip. Be sure not to go hashtag crazy. Just a few will do. And last, don't include punctuation in your hashtags, such as the apostrophe in "don't," otherwise, your hashtag phrase stops where you insert the punctuation.

Our Relationship Has Just Begun So This is Not Goodbye

So here we are … we've made it to the conclusion. But conclusion doesn't mean it's over. In fact, for our purposes, your journey here is just beginning. Now you have a roadmap to follow on this journey, so that rather than wandering aimlessly through the social media landscape, you can enter this phase of building your business with confidence and a plan. Throughout this book, we've taught you about:

- Strategy
- Understanding the landscape
- Understanding of resources
- Plan of action
- Building your content calendar
- Measuring and pivoting for success

Remember, the fundamentals you've now learned are very important and are pivotal to the success or failure of your efforts and investment. Your hard work will determine your success, but having a plan toward your goals is half the battle. Keep your content strategy in perspective and use the tools we've provided, and you'll be well on your way to building your book of business.

But our journey together doesn't end here. Instead, I am prepared to be here to help you along the way. As we said, this is not the end, but rather the beginning. We will continue our dialogue about building your business vis a vis your content and social strategy both on our website and on our social media pages.

Throughout this book, I've directed you to look to my website for deeper resources and further information. That offer will continue well past the time it took you to read this book. I will be continuously updating our tools and templates to bring you the most up-to-date and relevant tools to use as you work through this process. Social platforms change and morph all the time, and we'll update our tools and information as they do, so check back often for new information and updated tools. And of course, I'll keep you updated with my newsletter. We encourage you to share your stories with us on Facebook, Twitter, and LinkedIn of how these tools and tips and tricks we've shown you here have worked for you, and your successes in transforming this plan of action into successful business growth and revenue.

I also have a gift for you for making it this far. I know how hard it is to gain momentum, so I've put together 25 Content Ideas to help get you started available on my website.

I look forward to hearing about your successes and helping you along the way toward the socially savvy and successful legal practice you now have the building blocks to build. Let's stay in touch!

Michele Ruiz
www.MicheleRuiz.com
Twitter: @MicheleRuiz01
Facebook: Michele Ruiz
LinkedIn: Michele Ruiz
Google+: Michele Ruiz
Instagram: Michele Ruiz

End Notes

1. Brad Friedman, "76 Percent Look to Internet When Hiring an Attorney," *The Fried Side Blog,* October 3, 2012, https://friedmansocial-media.com/76-percent-look-to-internet-when-hiring-attorney
2. "How Today's Consumers Really Search for an Attorney," LexisNexis, October 23, 2012, http://cdn.lawyerist.com/lawyerist/wp-content/uploads/2012/11/How_Todays_Consumers_Really_Search_for_an_Attorney_102312.pdf
3. Shea Bennett, "How are Lawyers Using Social Media?", *Social Times,* February 20, 2015, http://www.adweek.com/socialtimes/lawyers-social-media/615605
4. Greentarget, ALM Legal Intelligence, and Zeughauser Group, "2014 State of Digital and Content Marketing Survey," http://www.digitalandcontentsurvey.com/wp-content/uploads/2015/09/2014-Survey.pdf
5. "Global Trust in Advertising and Brand Messages," *Nielsen,* April 10, 2012, http://www.nielsen.com/us/en/insights/reports/2012/global-trust-in-advertising-and-brand-messages.html
6. Sandi Fox, "As Zimmerman Surrenders, Is Social Media a Game Changer for Defense Attorneys?", *PBS Newshour,* June 3, 2012. http://www.pbs.org/newshour/rundown/as-zimmerman-surrenders-is-social-media-a-game-changer-for-defense-attorneys
7. Michael E. Lackey Jr. and Joseph P. Minta, "Lawyers and Social Media: The Legal Ethics of Tweeting, Facebooking, and Blogging, *Touro Law Review,* Vol. 28, No. 1, July 18, 2012, Accessed July 31, 2015, http://digitalcommons.tourolaw.edu/cgi/viewcontent.cgi?article=1138&context=lawreview
8. Louis Hansen, "Ex-Norfolk Prosecutor Charged Over Facebook Posts," *The Virginian-Pilot,* July 27, 2012, http://hamptonroads.com/2012/07/exnorfolk-prosecutor-charged-after-facebook-post

9. John G. Browning, "Prosecutorial Misconduct in the Digital Age," *Albany Law Review*, Vol 77.3, October 7, 2014, http://www.albanylawreview. org/Articles/Vol77_3/77.3.0881%20Browning.pdf

10. "In the Matter of Dannitte Mays Dickey," *South Carolina Judicial Department*, Opinion 27090, February 1, 2012, http://www.sccourts. org/opinions/displayOpinion.cfm?caseNo=27090

11. Jason Riley, "Judge Reprimanded for 'Liking' Attorney Facebook Pages," *WDRB.com*, December 22, 2014, http://www.wdrb.com/story/ 27689917/judge-reprimanded-for-liking-attorney-facebook-pages

12. Cara E. Greene, "Competent Representation: Ethics and Technology in the Practice of Law, *American Bar Association*, April 2013, http://www. americanbar.org/content/dam/aba/events/labor_law/2013/04/aba_ national_symposiumontechnologyinlaboremploymentlaw/16_greene. authcheckdam.pdf

13. Melissa F. Brown, Josh King, and Christina L. Angell (mod.), "Legal Ethics of Social Media," *American Bar Association*, 2014, http://www. americanbar.org/content/dam/aba/events/labor_law/2013/04/aba_ national_symposiumontechnologyinlaboremploymentlaw/16_greene. authcheckdam.pdf

14. Vanessa O'Connell, "Big Law's $1,000-Plus an Hour Club," *The Wall Street Journal*, February 23, 2011, http://www.wsj.com/articles/SB1000 14240527487040713045761603620287228234

15. Lisa Quast, "Company Social Media Accounts—Who Owns Those Twitter Followers?", *Forbes*, February 18, 2013, http://www.forbes.com/ sites/lisaquast/2013/02/18/company-social-media-accounts-who-owns-those-twitter-followers

16. Kevin O'Keefe, "Law Firm Social Media Strategy: The Five W's and How," *Real Lawyers Have Blogs*, August 27, 2012, http://kevin.lexblog. com/2012/08/27/law-firm-social-media-strategy-the-five-w-and-ho

17. "2014 Car Brand Perception Survey," *Consumer Reports*, February, 2014, http://www.consumerreports.org/cro/2014/02/2014-car-brand-perception-survey/index.htm

18. Allison Shields, "Blogging and Social Media," *ABA Tech Report 2014*, *http://www.americanbar.org/publications/techreport/2014/blogging-and-social-media.html*

19. Maeve Duggan and Aaron Smith, "Demographics of Key Social Networking Platforms," *Social Media Update 2013*, Pew Research Center, December 30, 2013, accessed July 31, 2015, http://www.pewinternet. org/2013/12/30/demographics-of-key-social-networking-platforms/

20. "Áudience Insight IQ," .*Investis.com*, Q3, 2013, http://www1.investis. com/~/media/Files/I/Investis-V2/pdf/publications/Investis-Audience-Insight-IQ-Q3-2013.pdf

21. Kevin O'Keefe, "75% Heads of State on Twitter. Law Firm Managing Partners?" *Real Lawyers Have Blogs*, January 2, 2013, http://kevin. lexblog.com/2013/01/02/75-heads-of-state-on-twitter-law-firm-managing-partners/

22. Duggan and Smith, *SMU.*

23. Tim Perzyk, "Survey: How Small and Medium-Sized Businesses Benefit from their Twitter Presence," *Twitter.com*, August 22, 2013, https://blog.twitter.com/2013/survey-how-small-and-medium-sized-businesses-benefit-from-their-twitter-presence

24. "Number of Monthly Active Facebook Users Worldwide as of 3rd Quarter 2015 (in millions), *Statista, The Statistics Portal*, 2015, http://www.statista.com/statistics/264810/number-of-monthly-active-facebook-users-worldwide

25. Maeve Duggan and Aaron Smith, "Social Media Update 2014," *Pew Research Center*, January 9, 2015, http://www.pewinternet. org/2015/01/09/social-media-update-2014

26. Monica Anerson and Andrea Caumont, "How Social Media is Reshaping News," *Pew Research Center*, September 24, 2014, accessed July 31, 2015, http://www.pewresearch.org/fact-tank/2014/09/24/how-social-media-is-reshaping-news

27. Andrew Perrin, "Social Media Usage: 2005-2015," *Pew Research Center*, October 8, 2015, http://www.pewinternet.org/2015/10/08/social-networking-usage-2005-2015

28. Substance Abuse and Mental Health Services Administration, *Results from the 2010 National Survey on Drug Use and Health: Summary of National Findings*, NSDUH Series H-41, HHS Publication No. (SMA) 11-4658,http://archive.samhsa.gov/data/NSDUH/2k10NSDUH/2k10Results.htm

29. John McDermott,"Pinterest:The No-Bro Zone," *Digiay,*February 20,2014, http://digiday.com/platforms/why-pinterest-is-still-a-predominantly-female-platform

30. Statistics, *Youtube, https://www.youtube.com/yt/press/statistics.html*

31. Lex Friedman, "Apple: One Billion iTunes Podcast Subscriptions and Counting," *Macworld*, July 22, 2013, http://www.macworld.com/article/2044958/apple-one-billion-itunes-podcast-subscriptions-and-counting.html

32. Tom Peters, "Presentation Excellence," March 19, 2013, http://tompeters. com/docs/PresentationExcellence.0424.13.pdf

33. Lev Grossman, "Person of the Year 2010: Mark Zuckerberg," *Time*, December 15, 2010, http://content.time.com/time/specials/packages/ article/0,28804,2036683_2037183_2037185,00.html

34. Kristi Hines, "What You Can Learn from the Top 50 Infographics of 2014," *PiktoChart*, December 1, 2014, http://piktochart.com/blog/ what-you-can-learn-from-the-top-50-infographics-of-2014

35. "Top 10 Things to Know About President Obama's Cuba-Related Announcement," *Latham & Watkins Client Alert*, Number 1780, Deember 18, 2014, https://www.lw.com/thoughtLeadership/LW-Cuba-policy-shift-announcement

36. Michael Stelzner, "Content Sharing: How to Build a Following Using Other People's Content," *Social Media Examiner*, December 5, 2014, http://www.socialmediaexaminer.com/content-sharing-with-guy-kawasaki

37. "Google+ Insights," *Google.com*, 2013, http://services.google.com/fh/ files/misc/insightsonesheet.pdf

Made in the USA
Middletown, DE
02 January 2020

82348181R00111